EVERYTHING ALL AT ONCE

'A tour de force critically examining the six simultaneous global transitions shaping our world... This book is a must-read to understand how the contemporary geostrategic, climate and technological flux can be leveraged to India's advantage.'

—**Erik Solheim**, former Executive Director of United Nations Environment Programme and former Minister of Environment and International Development, Norway

'Rajiv and Ishan have deftly delineated the six transformative global transitions reshaping geopolitics, economics, technology and climate. With clarity and conviction, this book outlines India's imperative to navigate these shifts with strategic foresight. A seminal work that blends intellectual rigour with actionable insight—vital for policymakers, entrepreneurs and informed citizens alike.'

—**N.R. Narayana Murthy**, Founder, Infosys

'Rajiv Kumar and Ishan Joshi have written a thought-provoking analysis of six global transitions that challenge the world today, and derived from their analysis a pathway for India to become a developed country, or *Viksit Bharat*, by 2047. The challenges they identify are the geopolitical and economic ones resulting from the shifts in the centre of gravity of the world's politics and economy to Asia, from technological change and the criticality of climate change. The authors' experience gives particular weight to their suggestions for what should constitute our ambitions to become *Viksit Bharat*, and how this might be achieved through reducing inequality and improving per capita income and living standards and quality of life. A book worth reading which should achieve its ambition of provoking serious and rigorous thinking about India's policies in a difficult and pivotal moment.'

—**Shivshankar Menon**, former National Security Advisor and Foreign Secretary

'Rajiv Kumar and Ishan Joshi have deployed their formidable analytical skills and impressive professional credentials to pen an outstanding book. *Everything All At Once: India and the Six Simultaneous Global Transitions* is full of sharp insights, describing the nature and scope of the unprecedented global shifts taking place and how India could emerge as one of the key architects shaping the emerging global order. This will long remain an indispensable reference work for scholars and policymakers alike.'

—**Shyam Saran**, former Foreign Secretary

'This compelling book analyses six concurrent global transitions—including the geopolitical, geoeconomic, technological, ecological and ideological—arguing for a nuanced, strategic response from India. Advancing a holistic development paradigm that balances economic growth with environmental sustainability and social equity, it is a timely contribution to policy discourse and offers a rigorous blueprint for *Viksit Bharat*. A worthwhile read.'

—**Amit Chandra,** Founder, ATE Chandra Foundation, and Founder and Governing Board Member, Ashoka University

'The call for a new development paradigm in this important book must be heeded by every thinking Indian. Its comprehensive understanding of the transitions taking place in the world, from climate change to technology, is the foundation to shape the discourse on India's future. An essential read.'

—**Sundeep Waslekar**, President, Strategic Foresight Group, and author of *A World Without War*

'A very accessible and compelling read for the layman and expert alike. A crystal-ball roadmap for India's bright future!'

—**Kevin Stanton**, former Chief Services Officer, Mastercard

EVERYTHING ALL AT ONCE

India and the Six Simultaneous Global Transitions

RAJIV KUMAR
ISHAN JOSHI

RUPA

Published by
Rupa Publications India Pvt. Ltd 2025
7/16, Ansari Road, Daryaganj
New Delhi 110002

Sales centres:
Bengaluru Chennai
Hyderabad Jaipur Kathmandu
Kolkata Mumbai Prayagraj

P-ISBN: 978-93-7003-923-0
E-ISBN: 978-93-7003-904-9

First impression 2025

10 9 8 7 6 5 4 3 2 1

Printed in India

To our grandchildren: Sai, Amaira, Ishir and Riaan, who will inherit and lead the future

—Rajiv Kumar

To Sharmila: For everything, albeit not all at once

—Ishan Joshi

CONTENTS

INTRODUCTION

Crumbling Certitudes

The world is at a pivotal point. The stability of the international system, the welfare gains of globalization, the universal recognition of the need to respect planetary boundaries, and the consensus on the deployment of technology for the common good seem to be passé. Neo-nationalism is on the rise, and the global economy is on the edge of a hyper-protectionist precipice led by the US under President Donald Trump. The old order is crumbling, and the changes being wrought in its wake have raised existentialist questions.

This state of affairs, we argue, emanates from the six global transitions that are currently underway simultaneously. Each of the transitions is profoundly consequential in itself. Taken together, with everything happening all at once, as it were, they promise to be epochal. Nation-states, the primary agents of global interaction covering the gamut of cooperation, competition and confrontation between countries, will have to adapt to these transitions to optimize their respective development trajectories. The more resourceful nation-states are already seeking to influence them to their advantage.

These historically unprecedented transitions may broadly be

identified as: (i) the geopolitical transition; (ii) the geographical transition of the global centre of gravity from the transatlantic region back to the Indo-Pacific region after a hiatus of two centuries; (iii) the geoeconomic transition; (iv) the transition of economic power away from Organisation for Economic Co-operation and Development (OECD) countries to the emerging economies of the Global South; (v) the transformative technological transition engendered by the artificial intelligence (AI)-led digital revolution; and (vi) the critical transition from carbon neutrality to reducing carbon footprint, and carbon removal from the environment.

Further, the six simultaneous transitions are unfolding against the backdrop of:

(i) The United States (US) remaining the most powerful and prosperous nation in the world with a GDP of \$29.16 trillion in 2024.[1] Before Trump, the US achieved a growth of over 3.5 per cent over the past three years (2022, 2023 and 2024), defying all consensus forecasts hinting at a sharp contraction in economic activity consequent upon the rise in interest rates as part of the US Federal Reserve's fight against inflation.

(ii) China staying firmly in second place, with a GDP of \$18.27 trillion in 2024,[2] despite a stuttering post-Covid economic recovery. The Chinese economy is, quite astonishingly, already more than four times the third-ranked German economy, and nearly six times the Indian economy.

(iii) The great resilience demonstrated by the Euro region after the initial severe shock in energy supplies and prices due to Russia's invasion of Ukraine.

(iv) Emerging economies gaining heft in the global economic order, strongly exemplified by the expansion of the BRICS platform to include capital-surplus energy-exporting economies of West Asia.

(v) The transformative nature of frontier technologies and the pluriverse of many possibilities they have opened up, which holds the potential to transform lives for the better or, alternatively, add an uncontrollable, chaotic and dangerous dimension to an already deeply inequitable and unstable world.

(vi) The rapid shortening of the climate change window to less than two decades in which to restrict the rise in temperatures to under catastrophic levels—which implies that carbon removal from the atmosphere has acquired criticality.[3] Mere mitigation and adaptation will not suffice.

There is a widespread sense of unease in major capitals at the emergent fragmented world order. The sense of optimism which permeated the world in the decades after the end of the Cold War, despite lingering issues of power asymmetry and inequitable growth, has dissipated. This, in turn, is largely a manifestation of the unpredictability of the scenarios which may come to pass over the coming years depending on the trajectory of the six transitions. What is more certain is that Francis Fukuyama's bold proclamation that 'history is dead' was surely premature.

Indian policymakers must ensure that they are not seduced into tackling the ongoing transitions in either a piecemeal fashion or within a linear framework. We cannot be the blind men of the parable who each touched only one part of the elephant's body, and reached a conclusion on the creature's provenance.

Trump's Triumph

In January 2025, the accession of Donald Trump to the office of the president of the United States added more moving parts to the simultaneous global transitions which were, in any case, unfolding quite rapidly. Trump 2.0 has effectively put them in fast-forward mode. Given the manic pace and range of the policy twists and turns in the first few months of Trump's second term as US president, it appears that Washington is hell-bent on single-handedly hastening the end of Pax Americana.

It would be wise to assess whether this new normal in the US' external engagement will outlast the current administration's term; the early indications are that the consequences of Trump's pushback against decades of US internationalism will be with us for a while yet. What we are witnessing under the Trump presidency is not just an effort to reform global treaties and multilateral institutions through disruptions. On issues ranging from security, sovereignty and territorial integrity or expansion, to trade and tariffs, climate change, advanced technologies, and access to markets, not to mention critical commodities, the US appears to be in the process of tearing up the playbook which it had designed itself, and nurtured over the past seven decades.

There is no denying that the opportunity for, and (domestic) resonance of, this approach by Trump has been provided by the dysfunctional, unrepresentative and ineffective nature of the aforesaid treaties and institutions. We suspect, therefore, that terms such as 'Darwinian survival' and/or 'ultra-nationalist', which are in vogue to describe the evolving US strategic foreign policy matrix, may be inadequate.

There is something more primeval at work here in defining the attitude of the most powerful nation on earth towards the rest of the world. It lies in their deep ideological adherence to MAGA (Make America Great Again) and its insular victimhood narrative akin to that of religious fundamentalists. And the profit-seeking, transactional actions of the US administration are supported by a majority of the American voting public who are evidently convinced, at least for the time being, that their country has been hard done by for decades.

The supreme irony, of course, is that it is precisely the factors cited as exemplars by Trump as tantamount to the US, in effect, being 'ripped off',[4] which enabled its emergence as the world's leading 'rule-maker', and the acquiescence of large swathes of the globe as 'rule-takers' premised on Pax Americana![5]

Thus, on the evidence before us, it appears likely that Trumpism may outlast its progenitor, and the complete dismantling of Pax Americana could be an accomplished fact in the years ahead. The consequences of the US abandoning its universalist approach and global leadership role as we knew it, and the simultaneous rise of China, will have profound implications for India.

Joining the Dots

It is imperative, therefore, for Delhi to constantly monitor the evolving trends, scan the horizons to anticipate the unfolding phenomena, and adopt a nimble policy approach that will allow it to quickly respond and adapt to the emerging global conditions. In subsequent chapters, we discuss the nature of the six global transitions that are underway, and outline possible Indian policy responses.

Before we get to it, however, there are a couple of caveats to be entered in terms of how this book is structured. While high-quality academic work is available on some of the transitions or aspects thereof, which has enriched the public discourse, a meta-narrative is largely conspicuous by its absence. Ergo, the profound implications for India of the simultaneously unfolding global transitions urgently need to be understood holistically and fully before attempts are made to design a policy response. Thus, the primary objective of this work is to attempt to understand the characteristics of the six global transitions underway, the dynamic matrix which is emerging due to their simultaneity, and their inherent interconnectedness.

Only once the creature has been identified as an elephant, to revert to the analogy used earlier, and has been seen whole, can we address the question of the policy framework that could be constructed by an intermediate power such as India. The objective of the Indian policy response would be to adapt effectively to these transitions, best negotiate their adverse impacts, and where possible, try and shape the transitions to its benefit.

It is important to recognize that India is perhaps the only country in world history that has to tackle the twin challenge of significantly raising the welfare levels of its vast population and reducing its carbon footprint *at the same time*. The simultaneity of the multiple transitions that are underway exacerbates the challenge.

Unlike all advanced economies which are now members of the OECD, or even China, we do not have the luxury of single-mindedly pushing economic growth without taking any cognizance of planetary boundaries. A major breach of these boundaries will result in a serious risk to our economic and, indeed, national security. India must, therefore, adopt a development paradigm that ensures both economic prosperity and ecological security.

The complexity and enormity of these challenges will compel India to design its own road ahead as it aspires to become a developed economy. Formulating such a development strategy will involve an intensive intellectual churning that will have to be persisted with for a considerable length of time.

This *Sagar Manthan* which must involve all stakeholders—government at all levels, private entrepreneurs and industrialists, and academia and civil society—will surely yield a new development paradigm for India. In the absence of such a construct, India faces the unsavoury prospect of being caught in the middle-income trap, and not achieving its aspiration of becoming a developed economy ('Viksit Bharat') by 2047, thereby being guilty of responding sub-optimally to the aspirations of its populace. As it unfolds, and is successfully implemented, this Indian development paradigm could become an exemplar for other emerging economies facing a similar set of challenges.

Our attempt here is but a first step in evolving such a paradigm. But it is also a necessary step, if only to initiate the churning, or *manthan*, required for developing a framework to successfully address the multiple and simultaneous global transitions.

ONE

PAX AMERICANA, QUO VADIS!

Geopolitical Transition

Geopolitical transitions have been a feature of the modern world since the rise of Pax Britannica in the nineteenth century, until its demise with the Allied powers' victory over Nazi Germany in the Second World War. From an empire on which the sun never set, Britain became a junior partner to the US with the rise of Pax Americana in the post-war era.

This chapter traces the rise of Pax Americana from the end of the Second World War until it reached its zenith with the emergence of a unipolar world which was coterminous with the collapse of the Soviet Union in 1991. We then discuss the unipolar years after 1991, highlighting the US' self-adopted mission of creating a liberal-democratic world order which led, among other things, to Francis Fukuyama's premature end-of-history doctrine. Unipolar hegemony began to be challenged with the Russian occupation of Crimea in 2014, the failure of the US to impose its will in the Syrian conflict, and its inability to stop the Chinese from creating a new economic zone in the South China Sea despite opposition from the US' fraternal ally, the Philippines.

The contestation of this unipolar hegemony staged by both China and Russia over the last decade informs the next section of this chapter. China was, ironically, supported by the Americans for over three decades—first in a Cold War context, and subsequently in terms of deep economic engagement, beginning with the Sino-US détente in the early 1970s initiated by Richard Nixon and Henry Kissinger, and extending well into the twenty-first century.[1]

Beijing has used the enormous economic and technological

strength it thus acquired—which is now reflected in its considerable comprehensive national power (CNP)—to challenge US hegemony more overtly over the past decade. Russia, on the other hand, has not shied away from using military force (in Syria till the Bashar al-Assad debacle, and then in Ukraine) to push back against the US and its NATO partners.

The current period is, thus, one of massive geopolitical flux with uncertain outcomes. What is more certain is that the geopolitical transition will be a long-drawn one. For, the People's Republic of China (PRC) is highly unlikely to collapse the way the Soviet Union did. And the US, which has demonstrated the ability to rejuvenate itself from geopolitical and geoeconomic cycles, will try its utmost not to allow its hegemony to be degraded in quick time. Therefore, the ongoing churn provides larger operational space for intermediate powers like India to influence the possible outcomes.

We conclude by looking at the options and strategic space which could open up for India and other intermediate powers to navigate these turbulent times. The key for Delhi might be to focus even more sharply on building India's CNP and at the same time augment its strategic autonomy to be able to adapt to the evolving geopolitical situation with maximum flexibility.

The Evolution of Pax Americana

In a world where the intersection between economic and security interests has acquired critical mass, geopolitics is playing a vital role in shaping the responses of nations, blocs, multilateral institutions and international bodies to the shifts in the global balance of power. In the context of a diminished Pax Americana, there are numerous examples of the conceptual calisthenics indulged in by key players to ensure the preservation of their hard power.

Historically, US aspirations to construct what has been termed an 'empire by invitation' consolidated after 1945.[2] The Cold War's transatlantic peace order was the most significant geopolitical development of the last century, especially because of the speed at which it came about. The US took over the mantle of the leader of the West from the mid-twentieth century at a dizzying pace.[3] With Soviet-led states of the Warsaw Pact as its adversaries in the Cold War face-off, as well as Communist China from 1949 in its sights, the US doubled down on its global projection of power.

It bears recalling that the international economic order, with the Bretton Woods twins—the International Monetary Fund and the World Bank (established in 1944)—to manage it, simply reflected the preponderant US economic, technological and military power. This was evident from the 1940s, and continued through the period of the bipolar division of the world in the context of the Cold War.

The multilateral General Agreement on Tariffs and Trade (GATT) of 1947 began regulating trade among 153 countries in fulfilment of its charter to achieve a substantial reduction of tariffs and other trade barriers, and the elimination of preferences, on a reciprocal and mutually advantageous basis.[4] GATT functioned as a de facto multilateral institution, conducting eight rounds of talks addressing trade issues, and resolving international trade disputes. This continued until the Uruguay Round (1986–94), which resulted in an agreement among 117 countries, including the US, to reduce trade barriers and create more comprehensive and enforceable world trade rules, as well as the formation of the World Trade Organization (WTO) in 1995 to implement the agreement.[5]

In parallel, the establishment of the North Atlantic Treaty Organization (NATO) in 1949 added US military and technological muscle to its economic prowess and that of the West as a whole over the next 50 years. It would be fair to say that the creation of NATO was both a process and an event. It was the culmination of the post-war process of transformation of the US from a minor peacetime national security state to the security-intelligence behemoth it became, starting from the enactment of the National Security Act (1947).[6] But it was also the child of an event—the blockade of Berlin (1948) imposed by the USSR—which hurried the creation of the transatlantic military alliance as a counterweight to Soviet armies in Central and Eastern Europe.

Ironically, though, the one-for-all and all-for-one Article 5 of NATO—in which the signatories agree that an armed attack against one or more of them in Europe or North America *shall be considered an attack against all* of them, and they will respond to it collectively and/or individually—was invoked for the first time in 2001, a decade after the demise of the USSR. It came into play not against an adversary state, but non-state actors after the 9/11 terror attacks on US soil, organized by Osama bin Laden, killed over 3,000 people.

Yet, in the second half of the twentieth century, the most visible symbol of US military-technological might was NATO—and, for a while, CENTO and SEATO as well—which embodied Pax Americana.[7]

As Lawrence S. Kaplan, referring to NATO's operational head in 1982, wrote: 'The Supreme Allied Commander, always an American, was an appropriate title for the American proconsul whose reputation and influence outweighed those of European premiers, presidents, and chancellors.'[8]

However, with the collapse of the Soviet Union and Russia's growing integration with Western Europe, and the emergence of the global market-based economic order, NATO began to fray at the edges. In more recent years, Donald Trump, in his first term as US president, hammered in what at the time appeared to be the final nail in the coffin of America's image as the benevolent, generous, all-powerful security guarantor for Europe. The current Trump administration has continued with the rhetoric of its NATO allies having to do much, much more—and not just in terms of financial contributions—to keep the transatlantic security alliance going.

In response to this US pressure, their European allies have, indeed, upped their contributions to NATO, along with hiking defence budgets between the first and second Trump administrations, and even more significantly in 2025. As events since 2014 have demonstrated, Vladimir Putin's policies are redefining NATO's role as the guarantor of Europe's security vis-à-vis a belligerent Russia.

From a Unipolar World to Contested Hegemony

Following the collapse of the Berlin Wall in 1989 and the USSR in 1991, the world witnessed the emergence of a unipolar era with the US as the sole global hegemon. This lasted for 20-odd years. In fact, the emergence of the unipolar world can be traced to the early-to-mid 1980s, with President Ronald Reagan's characterization of the Soviet Union as an 'Evil Empire', along with Iran and North Korea. The implementation of policies aimed at destroying the Soviet state by imposing unbearable costs on it, is a part of US strategic folklore.[9] By its invasion of and subsequent debacle in Afghanistan (1979–89), the USSR did not help its own cause.

Meanwhile, the First Gulf War (1990–91) was an emphatic exhibition of US military-technological might, and its power projection ability, even in distant geographies. The shock and awe generated by precision munitions and tech-enabled weapons systems used by the US in the conflict were later termed a 'Revolution in Military Affairs' (RMA). The limits of US power, however, were also exposed during this period by a rising China. Despite being the only superpower, the US opposed but could not prevent the brutal crackdown on pro-democracy protestors at Tiananmen Square and elsewhere in 1989. It was an early sign of things to come.

Even though the evolution of Pax Americana continued into the second decade of the twenty-first century, the breakdown of Cold War politics, the relative decline of US military and economic capabilities, and the first stirrings of globalization had begun disrupting the international political and economic order organized around the territorial nation-state—the de facto unit of political order for a decolonizing world—much earlier.[10]

In fact, the advent of the twenty-first century proved tumultuous for the US as it fought the Second Gulf War, which arguably did not achieve its political objectives despite a decisive battleground victory. The US withdrew from a war-ravaged, splintered Iraq in 2011.

Washington also busied itself with promoting the so-called Arab Spring in the Islamic World with very mixed results. The ignominy of a Saigon-like evacuation of the last of the US ground troops from Kabul, Afghanistan, in 2021 after 20 years of fighting, which then saw the Taliban regime again take over the country with impunity, was surely the final straw.

It brought a sense of urgency to the long-delayed US pivot away from the region and towards Asia and the Indo-Pacific announced by Barack Obama in November 2011. But China had already inveigled itself—through a combination of coercion, confrontation and cooperation—into the economic and security domains of numerous Southeast Asian states by the time the US got around to acting on its Indo-Pacific pivot.

Washington would also pay a strategic price over the next decade for its less-than-robust responses, for example, to Putin's invasion of Georgia (2008) and the annexation of Crimea (2014), and the Chinese creation of artificial islands in the contested South China Sea, which also took place in 2014.[11,12]

While a Putin-led Russia showed its hand in Crimea, a Xi Jinping-led China, which had assiduously augmented its CNP over the past three decades, decided that it had finally gone beyond Deng Xiaoping's dictum to keep its sights lowered, and began asserting its position in the Asia-Pacific region.[13]

Sino-US Competition: A Great Power Rivalry

Over a decade ago, Randall Schweller and Xiaoyu Pu, in their influential monograph *After Unipolarity: China's Visions of International Order in an Era of US Decline*, iterated: 'China does not yet have a fixed blueprint for a new world order. Instead, competing Chinese visions of order map on to various de-legitimation strategies and scenarios about how the transition from unipolarity to a restored global balance of power will develop.'[14]

More recently, as Nabarun Roy's essay examining the role of realism in the study of international relations underlines, 'though moving away from a strict neoclassical realist schema, [Schweller and Pu] use James Scott's insights pertaining to resistance by subordinate groups under conditions of hegemony, to understand the de-legitimisation of US hegemony by China.'[15]

The Sino-US rivalry will clearly remain the defining feature of the ongoing geopolitical transition even as a group of eight to ten intermediate powers, including India, with their increasing strategic heft, are also beginning to play a role as influencers in the global system.

US recognition of this reality is exemplified by Washington strategically pivoting from the AF-Pak or West Asian region to the Indo-Pacific under Barack Obama's presidency, establishing the AUKUS security alliance, expanding the scope of the Quad, nudging Japan to focus on bolstering its military capabilities, renewing efforts to strengthen security and economic ties with ASEAN, and significantly upping military-technology engagement with India.

The emergent Sino-US rivalry, though, is a very different beast when compared to the strategic competition the US and the former USSR engaged in across domains for the better part of the twentieth century. There is no Cold War redux with two clean-cut economic blocs à la COMECON versus the US-EEC. Despite the elevated rhetoric on decoupling and/or derisking, US and China are still tied at the hip economically.

In the mutually profitable economic engagement between the two twenty-first century adversaries, the US' total goods trade with China was worth an estimated $582.4 billion in 2024. US goods exports to China in 2024 were $143.5 billion, down 2.9 per cent ($4.2 billion) from 2023. US goods imports from China in 2024 totalled $438.9 billion—an increase of 2.8 per cent or $12.1 billion) from 2023. The US goods trade deficit with China was $295.4 billion in 2024, a 5.8 per cent increase ($16.3 billion) over 2023.[16] US FDI in China was $126.1 billion in 2022—a nine per cent increase from 2021, while China's FDI in the US totalled $28.7 billion in 2022.[17]

But this relationship also represented a significant welfare gain for US consumers, who were the beneficiaries of cheaper goods imported from China. A large share of these imports emanated from manufacturing capacities created by US multinationals themselves in China. These companies have pumped in enormous volumes of capital for establishing these capacities. Although investors from the US, Japan and Taiwan now want to reduce the China country risk, it will not be a simple one-off process as happened with the Soviet Union. Any significant US-China decoupling as a result of their global rivalry will likely be a complicated and a fairly long-drawn process, despite Trump's tariff disruptions.

It is too early, also, to talk about the terminal decline of US as some have postulated. The US is still ahead of China in key CNP aspects such as GDP, defence production and military capability. The US remains the world's largest economy, and its influence is still pervasive across geographies and themes. This is in large part a result of the US dollar ($) firmly retaining its position as the global reserve currency. While attempts to replace it have now accelerated, with the euro gaining ground and China (with Russia in tow) and even India promoting trade and financial transactions in their own currencies, there is still a long way to go before the US dollar is toppled from its pre-eminent position.[18] The Trump 2.0 administration has made it clear quite emphatically that the US will do everything in its power to prevent this from coming to fruition.

Further, the three largest defence companies in the world are all US firms; the total contribution of the military-industrial complex (MIC) to the US' GDP is estimated to be—depending on which sources we rely on—between three and four per cent, including not just military equipment and technology, but also its broader impact. Prominent Chinese commentators such as Ding Gang had, as early as 2021, doubled down on the narrative that the US empire is bolstered by its MIC: 'The (US) arms industry directly serves the military. And the military of the empire is not only for the maintenance of defence, but also for the purpose of expansion and conquest of the world. Meanwhile, such industries in the US have absolute advantages.'[19] Because the post-war security system was established under the leadership of the US, Washington largely had the final say in terms of initiating armed conflict.[20]

Also, decades of focus on R&D had made the US arms industry

a world-leading one. A result of this dominant position was that when a nation incorporated US weapons systems and equipment into its defence structure in a significant manner, its dependency brought it into Washington's orbit. Quite a few emerging economies have become the US' fixed clients, and its MIC has become deeply intertwined with America's global strategy.[21]

While the US is losing its pre-eminence, it still remains the most powerful nation in the world, and the only one capable of transnational power projection. Its total military expenditure at $877 billion (2022) is still 3x that of China ($292 billion in 2022), and greater than the combined military expenditure of the next four intermediate powers.[22] The PRC, however, does have a massive defence budget which is second only to that of the US, and Beijing may actually be spending significantly more than it reveals.[23]

It should be underlined that while the US still has the biggest defence bill in the world, China's expenditure has grown the fastest over the past decade. Between 2012 and 2022, China saw an average annual increase of 7.2 per cent in its defence spend—the highest among the top 10 countries in the world.[24] The Chinese have narrowed the strategic gap with the US over the last 10–12 years, and are continuing determinedly to accelerate the pace of their catch-up. The PLA is rapidly transforming into an efficient, modern military, with large-scale adoption of RMA and digital technologies across the board.

While China is not close to catching up with the US in terms of aggregate power projection capabilities, it is a fact that China has overtaken the US in the number of patents filed, and in the development of some key emerging technologies.[25] Out of 64 critical technology categories, China took the top spot in 57 in 2024,[26] compared to 2023 when the PRC was leading the US in 37 out of 44 cutting-edge digital technologies tracked.[27]

Beijing is in the process of establishing a monopoly in areas like synthetic biology and nanoscale materials while it has established leads in fields such as electric batteries, hypersonics, and advanced radio-frequency communications (5G and 6G). The US is the clear leader in only seven out of 44 technologies—tracked over 2022–23 by the Australian Strategic Policy Institute—including vaccines, quantum computing, and space launch systems.[28] Xi Jinping's recent pronouncement of China needing to discover new production capabilities for powering its way out of the middle-income trap is aimed at further narrowing the technology gap between itself and the US.[29] China's overt goal now is to overtake the US as the leading science and technology player in the world.

The PRC has also been an early mover in Africa to ensure its energy security, as well as to acquire overseas military bases off the continent's coast, such as the one in Djibouti. Africa, always a rich source of commodities, has been extensively mined by Chinese companies for rare earths and critical minerals to secure a supply chain for renewables.

Rare earths are essential components for semiconductors, batteries, electronics, renewable energy technologies, and defence/GPS equipment. These are essential to the global green transition. Globally, China is clearly ahead in the acquisition of these assets. Beijing has a dominant hold on the market, with 60 per cent of global production and 85 per cent of the processing capacity of rare earths.

According to a Brookings Institute paper, the global demand for rare earths reached 125,000 metric tonnes in 2021, and is forecast to reach 315,000 metric tonnes by 2030—putting China in pole position for the transition away from carbon.[30] The strategic leverage this near-monopoly allowed Beijing was evident in its suspension of all rare earth exports in response to

Trump's tariffs in April 2025, leading to deep consternation in the US tech industry.[31]

In summation, it is both important and useful to undertake a nuanced comparative analysis of hard power—including the ability of the US and China (possibly with Russia in tow) to utilize economic and/or military prowess to shape global and regional scenarios beneficial for themselves. But this does not tell the full story of the multiple levels at which the great power rivalry is impacting the global geopolitical transition.

Cold War 2.0?

What of the role of ideology then? After all, on one side is an allegedly totalitarian surveillance state focused on the welfare of the collective, which places a premium on social harmony. On the other, there is the world's oldest democracy with a purported emphasis on individual rights, and an inherent wariness of state overreach in fashioning societal choices.

Many scholars believe this makes for a compelling argument that the ongoing geopolitical transition has most, if not all, of the elements that would classify it as Cold War 2.0 or a New Cold War. Especially as the level of economic integration between the two major powers is being subjected to policies aimed at diluting the concentrated risk by both Washington and Beijing.

The position that US-China conflict is driven solely by geopolitics as the PRC's rise inevitably clashes with the established superpower—the US—regardless of their respective political systems, had significant traction within Western policy circles till the turn of the twenty-first century. This stand was premised on the rational actor model of state behaviour, which implied that any geopolitical rivalry playing out in multiple domains was inherent and par for the course in the process of a rising power challenging the existing hegemon.[32] But the line of reasoning which has, of late, once again attracted more adherents is that many tensions would arguably be avoided if the US-led West was dealing with a democratic PRC.

Further, proponents of the decisive role played by ideology in the US-China clash assert that even if Washington chooses to ignore this ideological dimension—as it did, starting from the Nixon-Kissinger-engineered détente until fairly recently, in the hope that greater prosperity would result in greater democracy in China—the Chinese Communist Party (CCP) just won't go along. The conservative clique in the party already sees the conflict through an ideological lens, as is evident in both Beijing's language and its actions, according to Andrei Lungu in his essay 'The US-China Clash Is about Ideology after All'.[33]

Geopolitical conflict is more accurately mirrored, this argument holds, in the case of China-India relations. The Chinese leadership is not afraid that India wants to promote democracy and threaten the party-state's stability. For India, China could go democratic tomorrow and it wouldn't matter as long as the border issue remains active, Beijing continues to prop up Pakistan, and it persists with its policy of tightening the 'string of pearls' around India.

In contrast, ideological fears have always underpinned Beijing's and Washington's views of one another.[34] Deng's decision to strengthen relations with the US, like the economic reforms of the 1980s, was accepted by CCP hardliners as necessary for China to be 'rich and glorious', but never accepted as a path toward democratic transition. Deng himself characterized the pro-democracy protestors who were crushed during the 1989 Tiananmen Square uprising as the 'scum of the Chinese nation'.[35]

Conservatives in the CCP and the Chinese armed forces have long insisted that democracy was a Western plot to bring chaos to China by subverting the CCP and promoting Western values. The collapse of the USSR only reinforced this belief. The views of the conservatives certainly cannot be ignored, given that they have piggybacked on the rise of Xi Jinping since 2008 to ensure their say within the CCP decision-making elite. The Cold War 2.0 nomenclature to describe Sino-US strategic competition has parallelly been popularized in media outlets across the globe—spanning topics from manufacturing and military tensions to technology and Taiwan. This formulation is challenged by scholars who argue that it oversimplifies the complex reality of geopolitical and geoeconomic competition between China and the US which still prevails within the ambit of a single international system.

Indeed, in our assessment, it also elides the historical-structural differences between Soviet communism and what may be termed as socialism with Chinese characteristics—now purportedly practised by the PRC under Xi's leadership.[36] This itself emerged as a consequence of capitalism with Chinese characteristics, viz. the state-run market economy model emanating from Deng's famous cat analogy.[37] That the CPC has, since coming to power in 1949, pursued the Chinese national interest with a single-minded determination despite ideological, socioeconomic and geopolitical variables is a historical fact. In China, modern political praxis is thoroughly permeated with the nationalist ethos.

Unlike with the Communist Party of the Soviet Union (CPSU), there has been no serious effort, forget a call to action, for a so-called world revolution by the CCP even in its early years. The CCP has also not attempted to establish an institution comparable to the Communist International. The notion of Western-style internationalism—whether of the USSR-promoted socialist world solidarity kind or the US-backed free markets and democracy kind—is quite alien to China.

What the Chinese will do, as Bruno Maçães puts it, is tread their own path to progress, which will be distinct from the Western model of political society. Intuitively and analytically, the case for Chinese exceptionalism is strong—it is quite clear the PRC will follow its very own *Sonderweg* (special path). That being the case, where does it leave the rest of the world and its most powerful country, the US?

Christopher Blattman's 2022 work *Why We Fight* is often quoted in this context to suggest that the evolving Sino-US relationship displays several of the characteristics which can be causes of war.[38]

In our view, however, the China-US relationship will not be adjudicated militarily. Instead, as Ryan Hass writes, the crux of competition will be over which governance, social and economic system will prove capable of outperforming the other in raising the welfare levels of its population, while at the same time protecting its citizens from the adverse impacts of deteriorating environmental conditions.[39] Ideology will play neither an insignificant role nor an outsized one in driving the Sino-US rivalry.

The US can't be written off just yet—it has, through the course of its existence as a superpower, repeatedly exhibited the ability to reinvent itself. Therefore, we could witness a relatively long period of contested global hegemony which may result in either a messy duopoly or stable/unstable multipolarity.

The centrality of Sino-US competition to the geopolitical transition underway thus cannot be wished away. Both intermediate and smaller powers are worried about the impact, especially economic, of being caught in the middle of another great power rivalry. Pax Americana is under severe pressure not only from external sources but indeed from its internal sociopolitical dynamics as well.

The international order underwritten by the US and safeguarded by its dominant military power is in the throes of a significant change. The ongoing geopolitical transition could be interpreted as suggesting that policy design premised on the study of the past may not be sufficient to determine the preparedness to negotiate the emerging global order. This is especially true in a setting where epochal and transformative technological and carbon transitions, among the other five, are unfolding simultaneously.

At a time when the geopolitical volatility index is at an all-time high as it is now, the trajectory and nature of these transitions will be critical.

Russia: An Actor of Consequence

An illustration of the intense flux in global geopolitics sparked primarily, but not exclusively, by the rise of China, and its active contesting of US global hegemony, is the Russia-Ukraine conflict which entered its fourth year in February 2025. The war disrupted global supply chains which were just about recovering from the Covid-19 pandemic—resulting in energy and food shortages and decelerated global economic growth—and caused a serious security scare in Europe. Yet, despite the destruction of lives, livelihoods and infrastructure, which is the tragic, inevitable outcome of military conflict, the world has not united against it under a single banner. Far from it.

Before the Trump 2.0 disruption, Washington and its European allies had been infuriated by Moscow's intransigence and persistence in prosecuting the war. They were also disquieted by Beijing's silence on the hostilities and its overt military cooperation with Russia. The intermediate powers also did not toe the US-Europe line, but adopted positions in line with their economic-security interests while making pro forma appeals for negotiations to end the war.

Putin, in an interview with American journalist Tucker Carlson on 6 February 2024, exhibited complete clarity about the political aims of his invasion of Ukraine. He did so while emphasising that US-led Western sanctions against his country, which experts agree will damage the Russian economy over the longer term, would boomerang.[40]

But Putin's bravado about Russia having been the fastest growing economy in Europe during 2023, and his not-so-veiled threat about the impending replacement of the dollar as the world's reserve currency given the greenback's weaponization by the US, may not be borne out in the coming years. (If China decides to put all its might behind a move to replace the US dollar as the world's default currency, however, the initiative could yet gain momentum, though this will mean an open confrontation with the US.)

The Kremlin's justification, self-serving or not, for altering national boundaries by use of military force in the second decade of the twenty-first century is the relentless eastward expansion of NATO. For Moscow, this is epitomized by the security alliance's backing of a pro-West Ukraine aimed at diminishing Russia. The arming of Kiev after hostilities commenced, and the vital military and financial support provided to the Volodymyr Zelenskyy regime by the West while sanctioning and emasculating Russia, were, according to Putin, a reflection of its desire 'to inflict a battlefield defeat on Russia.'[41]

For many, this turn of events is a confirmation of Russia's blatant intent, under Putin, to flout the international rules-based order to suit itself. But then, the actions of the Trump 2.0 administration are undermining that very international order as well. Further, there is no predicting if Washington and Moscow will come to terms going ahead. These developments are an exemplar of just how unpredictable and fractious the ongoing geopolitical transition away from Pax Americana is proving to be. Under the overarching theme of the emergent Sino-US strategic competition, there are numerous subplots playing out, with putative adversaries in one scenario emerging as potential allies in another.

In this situation, placing a premium on strategic autonomy as India, for example, has made no bones about doing, may be sufficient as a strategic placeholder. However, it ought not to be conflated with what India's defined position should be at the culmination of the ongoing geopolitical transition.

It was argued on the second anniversary of the Russia-Ukraine war by a Ukrainian diplomat that India had been one of the greatest beneficiaries of the rules-based international order, which allowed it to rise and prosper in a peaceful Asia.[42] The thrust of her argument was that should Ukraine fall, India would lose this stability. 'Taiwan may be China's first target, but in a disinhibited world, India's North-East, with its Assamese oil, would surely follow.'[43]

While it may be a sound tactic for the Ukrainians to emphasise the albeit limited gains for India from a Western-constructed international order, and the looming danger to it arising from a China-Russia pact, it is not out of place to underline that she was making an argument to attract support for her country. In using scare tactics in the prognosis for India vis-à-vis China, the diplomat was only doing her job—attempting to generate resonance among those simpatico to this view in Delhi.

At any rate, peace has proven fragile between Ukrainians and Russians despite being co-religionists, and with over 49 per cent of Ukrainians having family ties with Russians.[44] The two countries also had tight-knit economies until hostilities began. Let's not forget that Nikita Khrushchev was Ukrainian!

So, with a world order in the throes of transition, the possibility of the CCP attempting to bring to fruition its self-accorded mandate of restoring the glory of the Middle Kingdom doesn't seem all that far-fetched to many.

Yet, India needs to be cautious about buying into the China-as-bogeyman narrative, especially as our national interest may not be served by confrontation with our powerful northern neighbour at the current stage of our development.

This is not to imply Delhi should not keep a very close eye on the potential dangers of an expansionist, upper riparian PRC with which we have a live border dispute. India, after all, has only weak shared religious and kinship bonds with China, unlike those between Russia and Ukraine, and its economy isn't intertwined with the PRC's.[45] This is quite unlike Southeast Asian states whose economies are strongly integrated with regional supply chains that often originate and end with China.

But Delhi has to engage with Beijing for the sake of its national interests. India must begin to display the maturity required in recognizing that a freshly minted superpower such as China will look to constrain India's rise, including in its neighbourhood. For, as an uneasy duopoly takes shape globally, the PRC will attempt to protect what it perceives are its interests, and enhance its power projection capability. That is no different from what the US got up to vis-à-vis India and South Asia (despite being geographically distant from the region) during the Cold War and after. Until, of course, the economic liberalization in India and the subsequent George W. Bush-Manmohan Singh détente which produced the landmark Indo-US civil nuclear deal providing a fresh impetus to bilateral ties.

There is, therefore, a danger in being ahistorical when we bestow exceptionality on Chinese state behaviour towards India, because US policy towards us was equally, if not more, hostile for decades after Independence. From ending the supply of wheat under the PL480 programme in the late 1960s, to deploying the Seventh Fleet in the Bay of Bengal during the Bangladesh War, backing viscerally anti-India Islamist terror, patronizing military governments in Pakistan, promoting jihad in Afghanistan, and in more recent times, weaponizing human rights or religious freedom issues—policies that promoted perceived US interests have been accorded primacy by Washington. These were surely not supporting the Indian national cause.

Even today, with India-US ties having been elevated to a strategic partnership, and economic ties running deep, issues of technology transfer, market access, defence purchases and tariffs often come up as sticking points. The short point is: superpowers do what they do. The question for India is not which side to pick, but how to protect Indian interests by engaging with all sides while expanding our space to grow. That will necessarily mean analysing the end of the old order, and the emergence of a new 'multiplex' world[46] through a non-Western lens.

Meanwhile, there is no getting around the fact that the erosion of Pax Americana, which, in our view, is now being hastened by the Trump administration's neo-isolationism, has made the world more susceptible to conflict, including in the military sphere. While the intersection of economic and security interests retains its criticality in this respect, ideology also plays a role in the globally heightened risk environment, with deglobalization pressures intensifying and global defence spending surging to new highs.

In this context, it is educational to revisit the notion of quantifying disaggregated military strength. The combat power of an army has famously been equated by US military historian Trevor N. Dupuy to the product of three quantities: force strength (the number of troops modified by the quality and quantity of their equipment), operational and environmental modifiers (terrain, weather, posture—defensive versus offensive), and combat effectiveness.[47]

The last mentioned is the 'factor X', or the morale or spirit of the fighting force, which Peter Turchin and his colleagues in the discipline of cliodynamics have made progress in quantifying. Scholars in the field of cultural evolution have, in parallel, been probing the psychology of readiness for extreme sacrifice, using such concepts as 'devoted actors, sacred values, and identity fusion.'[48] Further, there's the investment in the implementation of deterrence strategies.

The geopolitical transition has, thus, taken current risk levels back to the period of uncertainty immediately after the fall of the Soviet Union, perhaps even to the height of the Cold War, or the situation in Europe in the late 1930s.[49] The world, as we will see in the following sections, is, once again, a very risky place.

A Messy Duopoly or Multipolarity?

The international order thus appears to be heading into an extremely fractious period, to say the least, with no global guarantor of order in a multipolar world. Issues affecting the world, from the environment and food and water security to energy access and trade, will be—and are being—impacted, if not weaponized.

The international system which emerges as a result of the ongoing geopolitical churn could alternatively be premised on bipolarity. This duopoly envisages the US leading most of the Global North, and China leading a large section of the Global South. Will it be 'messy'? Most likely.

In either of the above scenarios, the critical trends to watch closely would be:

(i) The evolution of the party-state in China, and whether it leads towards an opening up of the country and democratic reforms, or whether the surveillance state solidifies and an admixture of economic prosperity and assertive nationalism result in the perspective of the CPC staying unchanged as popular dissent becomes peripheral or is supressed

(ii) How successful the US is in reinventing itself, promoting innovation, and recalibrating its relationships across the world

(iii) The second-order effects of the China-alternative scenarios and the US-alternative scenarios playing out, particularly in the Indo-Pacific or Asia

The approaches of various countries towards conflict and security will also be based on the international system we eventually transition into; the Ukraine conflict has provided an early glimpse of how nations could stack up. Ditto, the American (re)involvement in West Asia in the face of China's growing diplomatic footprint in the region, and the Israel-Palestine conflict.

Over the past two decades, Russia under Putin has been pushing back against what it sees as NATO expansionism in its sphere of influence. Moscow, long written off by an influential section of the Washington policy establishment, is showing clear signs of attempting to regain its status as a relevant global actor.

Such a move, if successful, will significantly impact the geopolitical transition as the Sino-Russian alliance deepens with the latter as the junior partner, if not yet a client-state, of the PRC.[50] A potentially critical variable, however, has been introduced into the equation—Washington's direct engagement with Moscow, initiated in February 2025 as part of Trump's avowed aim to end Russia-Ukraine hostilities.[51] Additionally, Trump's stated position that Washington is also willing to engage with Beijing on issues ranging from trade to security, and China not ruling out such an engagement, would, if something substantial comes of it, increase the likelihood of the emergence of an international system premised on a Sino-US duopoly.

Russia and other intermediate powers, including India, would have highly consequential choices to make in such a scenario. In effect, if the US continues on the foreign policy path laid out in the first months of Trump 2.0, Europe would have to tackle Russia and India would have to deal with China largely on their own steam.[52]

A sharply focused examination, therefore, of theories on the rise and decline of great powers will be of signal importance. Such an analysis would include what the triggers are that would suggest that a rising power is facing structural obstacles in its ascendancy and/or a declining power is managing to arrest its decline, or at least the rate at which it is doing so. It would provide a theoretical framework in which a potential paradigm shift in the international system could be analysed and understood.

In doing so, a clinical assessment will have to be undertaken—of both the extent and depth of the US-China economic relationship, and whether the two nations can extricate themselves from each other in light of the rapidly expanding trade and economic linkages between the nations over the past two decades. It is also a fact that neither have global financial institutions been able to meet the needs and aspirations of a large number of nations, nor is there the will in major powers to effect reforms of the United Nations Security Council (UNSC).

The proliferation of regional security and/or economic groupings—from the G20 to the SCO, BIMSTEC and BRICS to AUKUS, IPEF and the Quad, and an expanded NATO—highlights the need for reforms of post-war multilateral institutions if they are to stay relevant in, or even survive, the ongoing geopolitical transition.

There are no signs yet of that happening, however, which brings into serious question the longevity of these institutions, and, perhaps more importantly, the shape of the alternatives which will emerge to replace them.

It is unpalatable for many, but the reality is that well into the second decade of the twenty-first century, nearly all armed conflicts between states are rooted in contested territorial claims. This has been brought home not just by the Ukraine conflict or, indeed, the Gaza War, but also by the status of Taiwan with the ratcheting up of cross-Strait tensions by China. There is widespread consensus that if there is a war between the US and China, it will be over the East Asian island nation.

While the history of tensions between the PRC and what it terms a 'renegade province', which it is determined to unify with the mainland, is not the remit of this book, the escalation of Beijing's rhetoric and intimidatory tactics vis-à-vis Taipei has the US and its East Asian allies deeply worried. In the context of the unfolding geopolitical transition, it also underlines the 'tyranny of distance' for the US. This gives China an edge if there was to be a full-fledged armed conflict sparked by Beijing acting on its thinly disguised and frequent threats to launch an invasion of Taiwan, if required, to effect a reunification.

The nature of the ongoing geopolitical transition is such that factoring in their respective long-term strategic objectives by both Washington and Beijing would militate against either side making moves that could lead to a full-blown war.

This is a conclusion arrived at on the basis of an assessment of multiple studies and projections of extensive war games. Nearly all of them are emphatic that a direct Sino-US military confrontation over Taiwan would yield pyrrhic victories for either side at best, and diminish both countries' CNP drastically.

But if for any reason both countries do clash militarily, it could fatally weaken both, leaving the field open for, say, a coalition of intermediate powers to make a play for global leadership. A US-China armed conflict may not only spread rapidly, but will cause deep damage to both countries' economic prowess, military capability and power projection ability. In an era of 'total war' wherein conflicts encompass cybersecurity, space, finance, social media and trade, as well as military aspects, and have a strong competitive aspect, the broad topic of security now includes data and markets.

For policymakers across Asian capitals, though, it's not just Taiwan which is tricky to negotiate in the Indo-Pacific region in light of China's growing assertiveness and the US pushback. The South China Sea maritime territorial disputes which the PRC has with the Philippines, Vietnam, Indonesia and Malaysia are a critical concern for the ASEAN. Other regional powers, including Japan, South Korea, India and Australia, remain wary of Beijing's ambitions in the Indo-Pacific.

There is a discernible sense of frustration in the Washington establishment that well over a decade after Obama announced the US' 'Pivot to Asia', the shift of strategic policy focus to the Indo-Pacific has not been adequately achieved. That this is the case despite the US expanding and deepening its bilateral ties with India, reenergizing relations with Japan, South Korea and Australia, as well as making strenuous efforts to regain the space it ceded to China in Southeast Asia, brings into sharp relief just how turbulent the geopolitical transition is proving to be.

In Europe, Putin is proving a far more pernicious and dogged adversary for the US-led West than many had bargained for. In March–April 2024, Russia launched a renewed military offensive against Ukraine timed with the US Congress passing a military aid package for Kiev. Putin also held out the nuclear threat if NATO committed ground troops to aid the Ukrainians.

In fact, Russia's invasion of Ukraine in February 2022 had followed Putin's announcement that Moscow was 'suspending its participation' in New START, the last remaining nuclear weapons treaty between the US and Russia.[53] The treaty, which took effect in 2011, is set to expire in February 2026.

Germany, a frontline NATO state in the face-off with Moscow, successfully weaned itself off from its energy dependence on Russia within two years of the Ukraine invasion. However, it remains seriously concerned about its security if it does more in terms of supplying the latest weapons systems to Kiev. The then German Chancellor Olaf Scholz said in March 2024 that he remained reluctant to authorize the sending of long-range Taurus cruise missiles to Ukraine, which the latter has been asking for.[54] The risk of Germany getting directly involved in the war obviously still weighs very heavily on Berlin.

The potential deployment of NATO ground troops in Ukraine, always unlikely, has become a very remote possibility now that President Trump is back in office. He has said he's willing to let the Russians 'do whatever the hell they want' against NATO's European member-states which do not contribute sufficiently to the continent's collective defence.[55]

The prospect of a transactional, isolationist America coming to fruition as the geopolitical transition results in pressures on the American economy and societal structures is real. The former President of the European Council has written that such a possibility makes more urgent Europe's nascent efforts to develop strategic autonomy and invest in its defence. The German defence minister had in 2024 itself begun speaking of 'decades of confrontation' with Russia.[56] At the heart of the debate on Europe's security is the question: Can the continent rest assured that NATO and the US nuclear umbrella will suffice, or will it need to operationalize plans to defend itself in the future as the geopolitical transition plays out?

The continuous conflicts in West Asia have earned the region the moniker 'a rough neighbourhood'. Today, that phrase could well describe Europe as well. This is not to say, however, that the theatres of conflict in West Asia are any less pivotal in the transition. These include Gaza, Lebanon (which has been pulled into the conflict as Israel seeks to degrade Hezbollah's ability to attack the Jewish state from the north), the Red Sea (where Yemen's Houthi rebels are running amok, primarily though not exclusively targeting Western vessels, along with launching missiles into Israel), and Iran (vis-à-vis which talks of a sustained US-Israeli bombing campaign have revived).

Multiple global flashpoints are contributing to hastening the geopolitical transition as it becomes evident that the US cannot be everywhere at once. Oil-rich and capital-surplus West Asian states are adroitly moulding their engagement framework with both the US and China, and a clutch of intermediate powers, to take the emerging realities into account.[57]

Significantly, these developments come against the backdrop of long-time American allies in the region led by Saudi Arabia and UAE seemingly unwilling to privilege strategic ties with the US over deepening relations with China, and diversifying their partnerships with a host of intermediate powers including Russia and India.[58]

Intermediate Powers, Increasing Space

The last piece of the geopolitical jigsaw puzzle is the role of intermediate powers in the ongoing transition, and both their capacity and desire to shape the future world order. The trajectories of and choices before these prominent emerging powers have immense significance for the world waiting to be born.

Russia, the second superpower of the twentieth century, finds itself diminished and losing some of the geostrategic significance it had for over half of that century. As the Sino-Russian alliance deepens with the former as the senior partner, Russia's attempts to retain its status as a relevant global actor through moves including, but not limited to, the invasion of

Ukraine, are symptomatic of the geopolitical transition which is currently underway.

Crucially, the risks for global stability associated with the deepening Russo-Chinese axis would require a deep understanding of Russian political structures, economic imperatives, and societal changes as they unfold.

The following factors imply that Russia will remain an actor of consequence in the geopolitical transition, at least for now:

- Its sheer geographical size
- Its role as an energy supplier
- Its attempts to bolster trade in the Chinese yuan instead of the American dollar
- Its nuclear arsenal
- The development of its missile (hypersonic ICBMs) and space weapons technologies
- Its cyber capabilities that have breached the best constructed security systems
- The potential of a revival of its institutes of higher learning (perhaps with an infusion of Chinese funds)
- The re-election of Putin as president till 2030

The deepening Sino-Russian alliance will have critical implications for India given that Delhi still sees Moscow as an ally on the global stage, specifically in terms of votes exercised in the UNSC.

Yet, whether on a bilateral (likely border) issue with India, or to counter the Indo-US strategic partnership, Beijing is likely, at some point, to turn the screws on Moscow vis-à-vis its ties with Delhi unless Sino-Indian ties improve significantly.

Uncertainties thus abound. Will Russian power over the longer term be degraded by the West to an extent that it becomes a client-state of China and/or its primary energy supplier? Will Russia's already waning influence in the former Soviet Republics in Central

Asia and the Caucasus become inconsequential? Will Moscow be able to exercise sovereignty on its eastern flank in a meaningful manner, or will Chinese commercial interests in oil make them the de facto masters of the region? As Russia's population sees a historic decline, will it become an existentialist issue for the country? What is the prognosis for a post-Putin Russia?

The answers to these questions will significantly impact the trajectory of the ongoing global geopolitical transition.

The momentous changes occurring in Russia's far east—ironically in Japan, the country which was the first Asian power to inflict a military defeat on a European power (Russia) in the modern world—are likely to be important drivers of the geopolitical transition.

Japan's policymaking focus is now clearly on mitigating the increasingly severe regional security challenges to the country. It is doing so by closely aligning itself with its longstanding ally, the US, and coordinating with countries such as Australia and India within the upgraded Quad, with which Tokyo sees a convergence of interests as the cornerstone of its security policy in the Indo-Pacific. Japan's 2022 National Security Strategy took a huge step towards making Japan a 'normal' world power by approving dramatic changes to its decades-old policy of military restraint.[59]

Tokyo said it would significantly increase its defence spending by 2027—though there is debate on whether it is a 'doubling' of the military budget, or a hike of something between 56 per cent and 65 per cent—adding about $315 billion to its national security spend over the next three-odd years.[60] Japan has also committed itself to developing a new 'counterstrike capability' enabling it to conduct retaliatory attacks on enemy territory; it's an unprecedented move as it allows overseas deployment of its forces and marks a remarkable departure from its previous policy.

Taken collectively, these moves signal a transformation which amounts to Japan rearming itself, and reflect a consensus in Tokyo on the failure of Article 9 of Japan's pacifist Constitution to influence the successive military budget increases by China, the Russian invasion of Ukraine, and North Korea amassing weapons of mass destruction. These developments also indicate that despite the continuing challenges for Japan, including the non-inclusion of women in sociopolitical power structures, an ageing population, resistance to immigration as family sizes decline or remain stagnant, and sub-par innovation levels, the country is making concerted efforts to at least punch its weight in shaping the geopolitical order.

Tokyo is paying greater attention to business reinvention and digital transformation, and steadily reinforcing a role for itself in Indo-Pacific digital trade rule-making. That Japan, along with redefining its security strategy, is attempting to make its universities more diverse, promote societal acceptance of immigration, and play a more active diplomatic role in the region, indicates—especially given the power of Japanese capital—that the policies it adopts going forward could significantly influence the geopolitical transition.

As the great power rivalry intensifies, its second-order effects are proving to be the most acute in the Indo-Pacific. The region's waterways are vital to global trade, the PRC's energy security, and US efforts at curtailing China's strategic footprint.

Indonesia, with its growing economic heft and emphasis on maintaining its strategic autonomy, is emerging as a power with the capacity to play a major role in the geopolitical transition. It is the sixth biggest emerging market by GDP, and in the past decade, has grown faster than any other $1 trillion-plus economy bar China and India. The sprawling Southeast Asian nation—the world's third-largest electoral democracy and largest

Muslim-majority country—has made impressive gains since the fall of Suharto's authoritarian regime in 1998.

A source of dynamism for Indonesia is digital services, which are helping create a more integrated consumer market with over 100 million people collectively spending $80 billion a year on everything from e-payments to apps for on-demand trucking.[61] Another economic catalyst is Indonesia-specific. With a fifth of global reserves of nickel (used in batteries), the country is a vital link in electric vehicle (EV) supply chains.

As the West, China and India have increased subsidies to attract EV investment at home, Indonesia has spotted an opportunity. Rather than seeking to be the Saudi Arabia of the green-metal age, it is pursuing a policy of 'down-streaming'—banning the export of raw materials to force global firms to build factories in Indonesia. This is unorthodox, but over $20 billion of investment has already been secured, and the figure is rising. Coal-fired power stations are being retired early, pushing these new industries to run on clean, green power.[62]

In the security dimension, the Jakarta establishment has flagged the US-promoted AUKUS alliance as a step to the potential 'nuclearization of the Indo-Pacific' by setting a precedent in exploiting the nuclear naval propulsion clause in the Nuclear Non-Proliferation Treaty.[63] While this has been music to Beijing's ears, Jakarta has simultaneously been deepening its ties with the US following the elevation of the Indonesia-US bilateral relationship to a comprehensive strategic partnership in November 2023, and the Plan of Action 2024–2028. The two countries marked the 75th year of the establishment of diplomatic ties throughout 2024 under the aegis of the theme 'Diversity, Democracy, Prosperity', which highlighted cooperation between Indonesia and the US—spanning the spheres of security, economy, education and climate, as well as people-to-people interaction.[64]

Indonesia is also strategically located at a critical crossroads in the Indo-Pacific, which is home to vital sea lines of communication (SLOCs) and maritime choke points that serve as the economic lifeline of the Indo-Pacific. As a significant maritime power, Indonesia is therefore considered the de facto gatekeeper of the region which is a transit point for an estimated 60 per cent of global maritime trade.[65] Given such strategic stakes, Jakarta's role in managing the effects of the turbulent geopolitical transition on the Indo-Pacific cannot be underestimated.

On the other side of the world in Latin America, Brazil—the continent's largest economy which was once the undisputed leader of the world's most prosperous emerging-market region—is exhibiting signs of wanting to regain its status. The 'B' in the BRICS bloc has been, along with the other major economies of Latin America, a stark underperformer over the past decade, and more so owing to its sluggish and unevenly distributed growth.

Brazil figures among the world's top 10 largest economies, but has also become an exemplar of an economy caught in the middle-income trap.[66] To that extent, it offers policy lessons on what not to do. But that's changing, and the ongoing geopolitical transition has a lot to do with it. While China's maturing relationship with Brazil may have been initially driven by Beijing's efforts to secure critical economic interests, it could fill the investment gap in the Latin American nation leading to a strategic alignment.

That, indeed, appears to be the fear in Washington. The Sino-Brazilian relationship is at the moment perhaps in the nature of a pragmatic embrace, with the benefits of closer ties with China seeming to outweigh its costs for now. The fact that China has significantly expanded its influence in the Latin American region has contributed to the US having woken up to the long-term threat China poses to its own role as the leading power in the region.

Chinese customers now purchase almost 15 per cent of the

region's exports, of which Brazil produces a major chunk,[67] and the two countries have built an extensive trade relationship with total bilateral trade rising from just over the $3 billion in 2001 to over $44 billion in 2010, to $100 billion in 2019 and $160 billion in 2024.[68]

Brazil is yet to join Beijing's BRI despite growing calls to do so, but it now seems more likely than not. The bottom line from a geostrategic perspective is that if Washington is incapable of preventing Beijing from expanding its 'sphere of influence' even in geographically proximate Brazil, it would be confirmation that it's not just the tyranny of distance that constrains Washington's power-projection ability, but that a structural, long-term decline of the US may have set in already. The path Brazil chooses in the context of Sino-US competition over the coming years would be an important determinant in charting the course of the geopolitical transition.

Despite a degree of deterioration in domestic institutional structures, South Africa is widely recognized as the best placed country in Africa in terms of potential when it comes to human resources, value-added manufacturing, and technological expertise.

These are especially important attributes for the BRICS member-states, given the abundance of key commodities across the continent—access to which is a vital theme of the intensifying great power rivalry across Africa.[69]

A flourishing China-South Africa collaboration is reflected not just in economic ties—China has been South Africa's largest trading partner for 15 years in a row—but also in a strategic embrace. Pretoria has been using its clout across the continent, and within the African Union (now a G20 member), to support Beijing's 'win-win' BRI model and China's leadership of the so-called Global South to build an alternative to the West-dominated international order.

The close cooperation between the two countries in the recent expansion of BRICS, and the strengthening of parallel multilateral financial institutions, are illustrative in this respect. Politically, the post-apartheid ruling African National Congress (ANC) and the CCP have maintained close, 'anti-imperialist' ties. Additionally, South Africa filing a case against close US ally Israel for crimes against humanity in Gaza at the International Court of Justice (ICJ) signals the country's desire to challenge the US-led international order which it sees as unfair to African interests in particular, and non-Western concerns in general.[70]

It is for all these reasons that the second Trump administration has taken clear aim at South Africa, ostensibly due to its alleged 'government-sponsored race-based discrimination'.[71] As flagged earlier, concerted efforts in Africa by Beijing for over two decades have resulted in the establishment of a fairly sound energy–rare earths–critical minerals security architecture for China, as well as provided it access to overseas bases.

In recent times, it is South Africa that has been aiding these Chinese efforts on the continent while continuing to engage with Western powers. Given its unique leadership position at sub-regional and continental levels, South Africa's tilt towards China will substantively impact the global geopolitical transition as Africa, the world's youngest continent with a median age of just 19, will also be home to 25 per cent of the world's total population and one-third of the youth (15–24 years) population by 2050.[72] The infusion of Chinese capital into vital infrastructure has not only enhanced the PRC's strategic footprint, but also contributed to making the African youth bulge productive in some regions.

Before Trump 2.0, US policymaking adopted a twin-track approach to counter China in Africa. First, Washington pushed a narrative denigrating Beijing's mercantilist approach to achieving its strategic aims. Secondly, the US was working towards a new, more flexible regional policy premised on fostering open societies; delivering democratic and security dividends; advancing post-pandemic recovery and economic opportunities; and supporting conservation, climate adaptation, and an equitable energy transition process. But these are processes, not events. The Trump administration may possibly seize upon the fact that there is, as yet, not much evidence to show that the US approach hitherto adopted has gained any traction. This may well set the stage for a neo-transactional US policy framework vis-à-vis Africa.

In South Africa, as in other parts of the continent over the past few years, there have been intermittent, violent protests over the rising cost of food. Global institutions in debt relief negotiations have required African countries to slash subsidies on food, fuel and fertilizers, which has sparked renewed fears that mass discontent over food prices would continue to grow.

If such a situation continues, it could well push South Africa and other prominent nations further into the arms of the Chinese, despite the well-recognized dangers of Beijing's debt diplomacy. As the geopolitical transition evolves, South Africa is likely to be under growing pressure given the African continent's projected demographic profile which can be either a source of massive instability or a springboard to security and prosperity over the coming decades.

Intermediate powers other than those discussed above, including but not limited to Australia, Turkey, South Korea, Saudi Arabia, Iran, Germany, France, Nigeria and Argentina, are likely to be influencers rather than drivers of the geopolitical transition given their current trajectories. For over two decades, the sole global superpower was focused on the War on Terror. Today, significant US resources are committed to the conflicts in Ukraine, West Asia and, of course, the grand effort to resist the inexorable rise of China.

The 2022 US National Security Strategy identified the PRC as the US' only competitor, with both the intent to reshape the international order and, increasingly, the economic, diplomatic, military and technological power to do so.[73] The US National Defense Strategy, issued earlier in 2022, reiterated that the PRC is the country's most consequential strategic competitor and the pacing challenge for the US Department of Defense.[74]

The diminution of Pax Americana has corresponded with an escalation of internal and external conflicts across the globe. These multiple sources of conflict tie up the resources of even the world's biggest economy and strongest military power, raising the spectre of US *overstretch*.

China's strategic foreign policy appears aimed at exploiting precisely this situation—the PRC has begun making inroads into domains and geographies that were once considered exclusive US preserves.

American efforts to get its pact allies and non-pact partners to share in the heavy-lifting to meet the cross-domain challenges posed by the Sino-Russian axis have met with a sub-par response. That may be an outcome, at least in part, of the US clubbing both its adversaries together.

For India, attempting to negotiate the geopolitical transition in conjunction with the other simultaneous global transitions would require a careful parsing of its external environment before placing its strategic bets to ensure that the country acquires the space to grow. Diversification is the way forward.

Equally, the political will to continue the process of domestic structural reforms is vital. This is essential for growing and strengthening the domestic economy which, in turn, is the necessary critical condition for effective diplomacy required for tackling the ongoing geopolitical transition.

Delhi's objective must be to respond to the fragmentation of the international order by strengthening its strategic autonomy. This can only be accomplished by exercising a laser-like focus on accelerating economic growth, and using frontier technologies to shorten the period of India's own transition to a developed economy.

TWO

ARISE, ASIA

Geographical Transition

Readers of a certain vintage would remember pouring over the day-late English county cricket scores published in Indian newspapers till the early 2000s. Today, cricket aficionados are hooked to the T20 Indian Premier League (IPL), which is one of the most lucrative sports franchises in the world. Country cricket is now a boutique play while the IPL is a magnet for capital investment.

Alternatively, think of the thirteenth-century Venetian merchant-adventurer Marco Polo who travelled audaciously along the Silk Road braving all manner of dangers. His writings are widely credited with providing the West with its first comprehensive look at the cultural, economic and political structures of China, India, Japan and other Asian societies. Cut to contemporary times. China's Belt and Road Initiative (BRI) is a breathtakingly ambitious effort to remake the East–West connection, but on its own terms!

These are but two examples of the ongoing shift in the global balance of power from the transatlantic to the Asia-Pacific.

Indeed, when the Barack Obama administration announced the US' 'Pivot to Asia' in November 2011,[1] it was a formal recognition by the world's most powerful nation of an emerging reality: That a reversion to mean was underway, with the global centre of gravity shifting back to the pre-colonial period powers, especially in Asia, from the Western powers.

Obama's policy shift was informed by the rise of China over the previous two decades, and the realization that the American preoccupation with the Middle East might no longer serve the US national interests. This geographical transition from the transatlantic to the Asia-Pacific has since gathered pace exponentially.

At the time, however, the pivot raised a contentious debate on what it meant for US foreign policy and grand strategy.[2] Some experts worried that the pivot seriously weakened transatlantic relations, left the Middle East in disarray, and dangerously confronted China.[3] Others insisted that vital US national interests had shifted in the past decades, and the pivot was required to address the 'Pacific Century and the threat of China'—that Asia was therefore where American military, economic and diplomatic resources should primarily focus.[4]

The pivot is now a *fait accompli*. But as Robert D. Blackwill writes in the *Lost Decade*, '[while] the literature on the US Pivot to Asia is extensive, very few examinations consider the 2011 rebalance in the global context.'[5] It is not just the US which is impacted by the rise of Asia. The defence policy, economic statecraft, diplomatic engagement, intelligence assets, and optimal distribution of national security resources of Asia-Pacific nations themselves and the major powers outside the region have also acquired criticality for the period ahead.

The significance of this steady process of a reversion to mean of the mid-eighteenth century for Asia cannot be understated.

In 1700, India accounted for 24.5 per cent of the world's GDP and China for 22.3 per cent, while Europe's share was 11.8 per cent (UK, France, Germany).[6] By 1750, China's share of the world's manufacturing output had gone up sharply to 32.8 per cent, while India's remained static at 24.5 per cent, and Europe's grew to 23.2 per cent. Together, China and India accounted for 57.3 per cent of the world manufacturing output in 1750, and if Asia is included as a whole, the total jumps to 70 per cent.[7]

Two centuries later, by 1950, the ravages of imperial conquests aided and abetted by the technology spurt engendered by the Industrial Revolution in Europe had reduced post-colonial India's share of global GDP to 4.2 per cent, with China faring only marginally better at 4.6 per cent. The US had emerged as the world's most prosperous country by far, with a 27.3 per cent share of global GDP in 1950, followed by Europe at 15.6 per cent.[8 9]

It is now clearly discernible that China, India and Asia as a whole are coming out of this 200-year blip—that is, 1750 to 1950. This upward trajectory is led by China's exponential growth from 1990 to 2020, when the Chinese economy clocked a 10 per cent annual growth on average over a 30-year period. And as Asia is on course to once again becoming the centre of gravity for the world after two and a half centuries of transatlantic dominance, the implications of the geographical transition are already showing signs of being far-ranging. In the geostrategic domain, the effects of the transition are being felt deeply not just in the region but well beyond it.

Suffice it to say that Asian countries and global powers are recognizing that from both the economic and the security perspective, this transition may turn out to be as strategically consequential as the historical—and historic—transition from the Old World to the New World.

In this context, it should be pointed out that national security establishments all too often work on the a priori assumption that advanced technologies applied in the military-security domain have, to a large extent, neutralized the importance of geography. Yet, as the literature on the subject clearly demonstrates, both technology and physical geography remain central to security challenges that will only become more severe as the competition between great powers of relative parity intensifies.[10]

It is worth underlining that the capability of a state positioned within a certain geographic region to rapidly deploy and sustain significant forces within the region is intrinsically greater than that of a more technologically advanced power projecting itself across a continent or ocean.[11]

Strategic New Normal

The Asia-Pacific is the preeminent geographical domain in which great power rivalry is playing out. The long-term strategic competition that the US and China are engaged in and the rise of a host of middle powers there—from India to Australia and from Japan and South Korea to Indonesia, not to mention dangerous outliers such as a nuclear-armed North Korea—are transforming the region.

Two of the most significant multilateral initiatives of the twenty-first century—the establishment of the Quad and the AUKUS security partnership—are both arrangements focusing on the Asia-Pacific. It is highly likely that the future global order will be decisively shaped in this region. Geopolitics and geoeconomics will play out in multiple dimensions, and their second- and third-order effects will produce complex competition, conflict, cooperation and (dis-)integration—all unfolding at the same time. A 'strategic new normal' is taking form, characterized by uncertainty, exceptional disruption, and unprecedented change.[12] As a recent research paper iterates, this new normal of the Asia-Pacific region is manifested in multiple patterns that are oftentimes overlapping and contradictory.[13]

US posture and strategy in the region draws from nineteenth-century and early twentieth-century debates going back to the writings of Admiral Alfred Thayer Mahan and Sir Halford J. Mackinder, which were based on their observations of physical geography and its effects on state formation, interstate relations, economic development and military prowess.[14] While Mahan's conception of geopolitics was deeply rooted in his navalism, with global choke points featuring prominently in his work, Mackinder advocated the thesis that modern technology would eventually negate the superiority of sea power. Both of them posited Asia—notably East, Southeast, and South Asia—as the global centre of gravity.

Ergo, Washington's twenty-first century construct of the meta-geography of the 'Indo-Pacific', linking it to the littoral areas spanning the Asia-Pacific and Indian Ocean Region (IOR).

The waterways of the region are vital to global trade, and to China for multiple reasons, including energy security, the emergence of China plus ASEAN as the world's growth engine with RCEP giving it even greater dynamism, and Beijing's strategic objectives in the IOR. China has an overarching concern that the presence of the US military and its allies in the Indo-Pacific island chains can cut off its trade and supply routes.

From Beijing's geostrategic vantage, its actions can be read as attempts to break out of this perceived encirclement. Westward, China's outreach extends through the BRI, aiming at the European market. Its side-arms in Pakistan (CPEC) and Myanmar (CMEC) are seen as ways to bypass the potential choke point in the narrow Strait of Malacca, which is critical for regional trade, and secure access to energy supplies around the Persian Gulf. Its expansion through a military presence in the South China Sea (SCS) is presumed to be in line with China's goal to enhance its strategic depth in the Western Pacific.

While China's neighbours feel threatened by these advances, the US perceives China not only as a regional and global hegemonic competitor but, as a commentator put it, also as the first military force on par since Pearl Harbor to press forward into the Pacific, approaching American positions on Guam, Hawaii and even the US West Coast. As a consequence, the US' diplomatic, economic—

especially in building supply chain resiliency—and military focus on the Indo-Pacific is unprecedented.

Washington's recognition of the critical importance of the Indo-Pacific is apparent. In recent years, the US has launched the Indo-Pacific Economic Framework for Prosperity (IPEF), revived the Quad, and established AUKUS. Its major non-NATO pact ally Japan is also attempting to carve out a role for itself in Indo-Pacific digital trade rule-making, and playing a more active diplomatic hand in the region.

Barring a force-majeure-inducing development, therefore, there is little doubt that the Indo-Pacific (or Asia-Pacific) region is set to regain its global importance and role.[15]

Referencing this ongoing shift in the global centre of gravity in an address to the Asia Society as early as 2017, former Australian Foreign Minister Gareth Evans described himself as an 'incorrigible optimist' (which is also the title of his political memoir). Evans said that he hoped the phrase aptly described 'how confident we should be about managing that environment [transition] in the years ahead, without too many tears along the way.'

He conceded, however, that there would be many sceptics. The reasons for the scepticism, he expected, were perhaps embedded in his speech itself, which identified the five big geopolitical shifts—all of them occurring in the context of the geographical transition to Asia in general, and the Indo-Pacific in particular—that 'most compel our attention.'[16]

To wit, China's rapid rise, the US' comparative decline, India's long-awaited emergence as a major player, North Korea's acquisition of nuclear weapons capability, and ASEAN's loss of a significant amount of its coherence and credibility at a time when both are needed more than ever before.[17] As objective 'tears-inducing' conditions for policymakers to negotiate, the five mentioned above constitute the perfect storm. Over the past half a dozen years, these have added layers of complexity to an already fraught-with-friction geographical transition.

It would be fair to say that both the US narrative of the Indo-Pacific as opposed to the earlier Asia-Pacific (when Washington still saw an admixture of cooperation and deterrence as a viable model to shape China's trajectory), as well as China's BRI, are exercises in power aiming to reshape the geopolitics of the region. Under Washington's Indo-Pacific construct, China is potentially excluded while the US' security border is extended to the Indian Ocean.

Beijing, on the other hand, has advanced the BRI as an alternative model of economic globalization and diplomacy that is characterized by open and fluid borders.[18] In early 2024, a group of scholars from the prestigious Chinese Academy of Sciences, Beijing, published a monograph in the journal *Political Geography* that captures the *zeitgeist* of what could perhaps be termed the Chinese approach to the ongoing geographical transition. Titled 'End of the Asia-Pacific: Geoeconomics, Belt and Road, and the Indo-Pacific', the paper deployed a geoeconomic lens using oil or gas and the solar energy trade to shed light on the Asia-Pacific's changing meta-geography.

In the words of the authors, power is constituted through relational coupling and decoupling as China and the US are locked in geoeconomic competition that expands but also contracts the imaginaries of the region.[19] Their findings suggest that neither China nor the US holds a relational advantage in all energy sectors—China, BRI projects, and the countries of the region are all significant importers of US oil and gas, while China's solar trade has accelerated regional integration that includes the US.

The paper concludes that China's exclusion from the Indo-Pacific is not consistent with the geoeconomic realities of the energy trade.[20] It is evident that the study has significant implications for other domains as well. To the extent that the 'construction' of a region is an exercise in power, the meta-geography of the Asia-Pacific or Indo-Pacific is a product of propaganda. It is worth recalling, as the scholars iterate, that in the 1990s, China's economic emergence was located as part of a broader narrative of the rise of the Asia-Pacific that would promote economic interdependence and regional peace.

By 2017, however, Donald Trump had replaced the Asia-Pacific with the Indo-Pacific—an acknowledgement of both the emergence of India as a regional power and its potential, viewed from Washington, to counter-balance an assertive China. Except in China, the term Indo-Pacific has caught on across the world, while 'China's inclusion is ambiguous, even absent, in the US-led Indo-Pacific.'[21]

Officially, Beijing has doubled down on its criticism of the US' Indo-Pacific strategy which, it says, claims to promote regional cooperation but actually clings to a Cold War mentality and zero-sum game tactics, (of) forming exclusive clubs. 'The real purpose of this strategy is to integrate small circles into a larger circle—an Asia-Pacific version of NATO—thereby maintaining US dominance,' asserted Lieutenant General Jing Jianfeng, deputy chief of the Chinese Central Military Commission's Joint Staff Department, in June 2024.[22]

The BRI, on the other hand, is also a fairly recent initiative and is positioned as an anti-colonial space by the People's Republic of China (PRC), which claims a long history for it; as articulated by Xi, it draws its legitimacy from the Silk Road.

Whichever side's argument one chooses to buy, it is difficult to disagree with the assertion that the Indo-Pacific or Asia-Pacific and the BRI are the two most prominent spatial expressions of meta-geography in the past decade and more, capturing complex processes of global relational interdependence but also relational exclusion.

An Opportunity Beckons

What is clear from the above discussion is that it will be critical for India to independently understand both constructs, and situate them contextually to arrive at an understanding of the intersection of geoeconomics and geopolitics that is the hallmark of the ongoing geographical transition. Designing a policy framework that can best leverage it is the key challenge for Delhi, especially as the IOR has emerged as a key area for both the US' Indo-Pacific construct and the BRI's region-making.

Far-sighted Indian policymaking premised on thorough analyses of the global geographical transition is of the essence if Delhi wants to, as it should, expand its strategic space in the region. The Indian economy has expanded significantly over the past 20-odd years, and has become more integrated with other Asian economies. Trade links between India and China have also grown. But, as Prof. Gulshan Sachdeva puts it, investment and connectivity links between the two Asian giants are still limited, and most other Asian economies are integrating with China and participating in mega trade deals like the RCEP and the Trans-Pacific Partnership (TPP) to improve their global value chains.[23] These trading blocs will affect India even if it is not participating in them.[24] Thus far, writes Sachdeva, Delhi's quest for greater strategic influence is not matched by confident foreign economic policies.

Instead of framing its economic ties with China in terms of 'decoupling' or 'de-risking', India needs to develop an independent economic strategy to strengthen its linkages within the Indo-Pacific region, including with the Chinese economy.[25] We agree with Sachdeva's argument that a lack of participation in the emerging Indo-Pacific economic architecture and attempted decoupling from China will likely be a self-defeating strategy. For India's strategic importance in the Indo-Pacific depends on its ability to integrate itself economically within the region, in terms of both trade and connectivity—the improvement of India's manufacturing capacity and exports is crucial for the success of its external economic policy initiatives.[26]

India's security and territorial concerns vis-à-vis China are valid and vital. But as the border détente agreed between Narendra Modi and Xi Jinping in October 2024 has shown, these are not insurmountable. The fact that this was followed by a visit from the national security advisor to China in December 2024 is an indication that the Indian policy establishment understands it cannot claim to be Looking East or Acting East if it can neither see nor engage substantively with China.

It is particularly important that India continues to stay out of the 2025 re-eruption of the US-China trade war while pursuing bilateral deals with both sides—especially as Trump's policies are subject to overnight change, and his raising tariffs on Chinese imports could also, at least in part, be a negotiating tactic. This implies that a Sino-American rapprochement is not as unlikely as some may think. India will be in danger of being left out in the cold in such a scenario, which is why working out an engagement model with the PRC—with absolute self-awareness that we are the lesser economic power by far, just as we concede the same in our engagement with the US—is of the essence.

This is not to argue that the complexities of the India-China relationship can be ignored, nor is it to suggest that competition between the two would cease. But there is no place for an inflated self-image if India seeks to leverage the potentially game-changing geographical transition which is underway in our half of the field. A once-in-an-epoch opportunity for India to reclaim its place in the world as it was prior to the colonial period—both in terms of hard and soft power—beckons.

THREE

IMAGINE THERE'S NO HEAVEN

Geoeconomic Transition

The pace at which the emerging-economy members of the G20 fulfil their aspirations of exponential economic growth, along with achieving human development indicators (HDIs) comparable to those of OECD countries, may well decide the contours of the unfolding global geoeconomic transition. The developed world and its denizens, having accumulated wealth inter-generationally, are now focused on protecting it when not writing about it. It is the emerging economies where the action is, as it were.

The contemporary global reality is that seeking mutual economic bliss-points is a fast-receding option for most nation-states and blocs thereof. A profound shift has occurred for the first time in the post-colonial world: Countries are no longer shy about emphatically recognizing and prioritizing their economic interests over those of others sans an ideological orientation.

It was not always so, as was evident through the decades of decolonization throughout the mid-twentieth century. The days of overarching global narratives—whether that of socialism being the answer to all economic woes or that of the promotion of laissez-faire as the ultimate growth panacea—are now well and truly over. History, with due deference to Francis Fukuyama, continues to be made!

Our modest ambition in this chapter, therefore, is to suggest ways in which Darwinian self-interest-driven state behaviour in the international arena—as the old world dies and the new world struggles to be born, to paraphrase Antonio Gramsci—does not make it a time of monsters.

The chapter is based, to that extent, on Angus Maddison's scrutiny of the interaction between today's rich nations and the rest to assess the degree to which this relationship was historically exploitative. This leads us to an examination of the driving forces behind the fragmented world economic order. These drivers, we suggest, are both a cause and a consequence of the geoeconomic transition.

As the developed world moves to a green future while attempting to enhance or, at the very least, retain its affluence, its proselytizing efforts in the cause of universalist ideals have come up against the reality of the aspirations of emerging economies for rapid and equitable growth, not to mention the Trump Effect.[1] Proselytizing apart, the actual behaviour of most advanced economies does not set a good example for those nations still in the throes of their economic transition. While going green out of choice and in the interest of citizens' welfare thankfully seems to have emerged as the developing world consensus despite US backsliding, rapid growth nonetheless remains non-negotiable if a significant catch-up with OECD countries is to be achieved and millions lifted out of poverty in the process.

The apparent breakdown of the Washington Consensus and the rise of civilization states that are charting their own economic paths and establishing rival institutions to the Bretton Woods twins are a vital component of the geoeconomic transition.[2] The WTO being in shambles also reflects the contested nature of the international economic order, and the necessity for re-designing it to suit current global realities.

The metamorphosis of globalization against the backdrop of the great power rivalry, the disruption of the world economy, and the rise of protectionism have together spawned multiple ironies. That the emergent Sino-US rivalry underpins the global geoeconomic transition is evident. The benefits to US and Chinese citizens and companies of the deep economic ties between the two nations following the 1970s Sino-US détente and subsequent Deng Xiaoping-led reforms are delineated here, and their respective trajectories as well as drivers charted.

Next, we examine the nuances and analyse the prospects of the decoupling and/or de-risking thesis currently in vogue, relating to the Sino-US economic engagement playing out. The effects of this recalibration of trade and commercial ties between the world's two largest economies are likely to be pervasive and profoundly impact the geoeconomic transition.

The direction and intensity of this transition will likely be determined by: (i) the nature of engagement between the two largest economies, i.e. China and the US, over the coming decades, and (ii) the role the major intermediate powers play in the ensuing transition. The rise of Africa, with its young population and vast mineral resources, will also be an important influence on the geoeconomic transition.

The chapter then takes a deep dive into the trends in global trade, which is now forecast to grow more slowly than global GDP for the first time in over 25 years. In the next seven years till 2031, global trade growth will be slower than output growth over a sustained period. This is symptomatic of rising protectionism and the risk of deglobalization.

The debate around trade must be an exercise in looking towards the future. The mix of countries, citizens and companies that stand to gain in the next era is changing. A better understanding of how the landscape is shifting will help policymakers prepare for globalization's next mutation, and the opportunities and challenges it will present.

The implications of the growing economic prowess of

developing economies, and how a combination of geoeconomic and geopolitical imperatives might drive the future of globalization—if there is one—are also analysed in this chapter.

The pre-Trump 2.0 world was divided into three mega trading blocs—the EU, the RCEP, and the NAFTA (replaced by the United States-Mexico-Canada Agreement or USMCA in 2020)—that were tending towards overtaking the spaghetti-bowl effect.[3] Despite the weaponization of tariffs, this still largely holds true. How, then, should India navigate global trade dynamics in this scenario? Will expanding bilateral trading arrangements with other countries be enough? Is there space and enough impetus for a fourth, India-led trading bloc to come into existence? These are among the questions we tackle.

Further, India's dogged persistence and reasonable success in simultaneously managing its difficult domestic three-fold transition—economic, social and political—combined with its commitment to tackling the environment challenge, make it an exemplar for other developing nations. This needs to be leveraged more effectively than it has hitherto been. The restructuring of global value chains (GVCs) post-2009 and the fact that a number of these changes house a digital technology component have significantly shaped the geoeconomic landscape. We address the challenges for India to integrate into GVCs.

We then present an outline of the global economy of tomorrow, and explore what India needs to do to successfully navigate its future trajectory through the ongoing geoeconomic transition. In this context, the critical issue of climate change—which may force nation-states to dramatically change their policies and even bring about greater cooperation among countries that would otherwise grow further apart—must be emphasised.

The issues arising from the ongoing geoeconomic transition will surely be affected by equally consequential transitions in other domains. Their cumulative impact will have to be assessed to formulate an appropriate policy response.

The central thesis of this book tying these multiple, differentiated aspects together is that there is no way to avoid the massive effort required to shape the simultaneous global transitions to India's benefit. This chapter on the geoeconomic transition underlines the imperative to think boldly about solutions rooted in Indian ground realities.

In summation, suffice it to say that if the economic heft in nominal GDP terms is the most vital aspect of CNP, and GDP per capita and improved HDIs are the bedrock of societal stability, the unfolding geoeconomic transition is sure to be very tumultuous indeed.

Circle of Unreason

A disintegrating global economic order in times of extraordinary geopolitical flux has intensified the competing—and often contradictory—interests of various stakeholders. This geoeconomic transition makes India's path to reclaim its prosperity and economic security that much more difficult.

Angus Maddison's celebrated work *The World Economy* pegs India's share in the global GDP at 18 per cent in 1850.[4] To reach that level from the present level of a mere three per cent share in global GDP, while at the same time reducing its carbon footprint, will be an arduous and historically unprecedented task for India.

To illustrate the disconnect between the developed and emerging world, let's take a dekko at the concept of a global circular economy. It is defined as one where products and materials are kept in use for as long as possible, then recovered so that waste and pollution do not exist by design, and where natural systems are regenerated. It undoubtedly has the potential to meet the challenges posed by expanding population growth, rapid urbanization, and the required growth in individual incomes and HDIs, especially for those at the bottom of the pyramid. But this requires that the resource intensity of future economic growth steadily decline over time—an issue that has been examined at some length by experts in recent years.[5]

The transition to a circular economy was deemed 'necessary' in 2019 by the United Nations Department of Economic and Social Affairs at a joint meeting of the Economic and Financial (Second) Committee of the UN General Assembly, as a means for accelerating the implementation of multiple Sustainable Development Goals (SDGs).[6] While conceding that the transition to a more eco-friendly economic system was complex, and required collective action by multiple stakeholders across borders, the joint meeting nonetheless reiterated that a circular economy was essential.

It is touted as an alternative to the current, predominantly linear, global economic model in which limited resources are unsustainably extracted, consumed and disposed of. However, progress on scaling such a model at an accelerated pace to ensure that the world is on track to achieve the 2030 Agenda for Sustainable Development premised on SDG 12, i.e. responsible and sustainable consumption and production, is still a far cry. Advanced economies are attempting to transition to this new economic model, while emerging economies and the least developed nations that are at different points in their development journeys are neither incentivized adequately nor have the capacity to do so.

As things stand, if the notion of a circular economy is the normative ideal, its realization is the prevailing myth.

The Washington Consensus, with its embedded one-size-fits-all approach and emphasis on free trade, a zero or uniform tariff global regime, unhindered capital flows, and large-scale privatization, is transitioning to a world in which the Earth's valleys and cleavages stand out in ever sharper relief as nation-states across the globe adopt a horses-for-courses approach. Even Thomas Friedman would agree that the ongoing geoeconomic transition confirms the world is definitely not flat.[7]

As the world economy transitions, is its dominant trait that of globalization in transition, or rising protectionism? That is one of the primary issues exercising the minds of policymakers across the globe. From the collapse of world communism in 1989–91 until the global financial crisis (GFC) in 2007–08, the world was undergoing deep globalization.

After 2008, a new, more protectionist phase of globalization began, one less open to global trade, which is now increasing more slowly than global GDP. The Boston Consulting Group (BCG), in its January 2023 report 'Protectionism, Pandemic, War, and the Future of Trade', reiterates that global trade in the coming decade will grow at a rate of just 2.3 per cent per year through 2031—less than the 2.5 per cent projected for global economic growth. This compares with about 1.5 pp of trade growth per percentage point (pp) of GDP growth in the 1995–2008 period, and about one-to-one in the 2009–19 period.[8] Rising protectionism in both developed and emerging economies, with a visible uptick in import substitution polices driven both by geoeconomic considerations and digital technology, are the order of the day.

India will have to face the unenviable option of having to grow its exports in a world in which 're-shoring' and 'promoting the local' threaten to further fragment the global marketplace. For example, the US Inflation Reduction Act (IRA) of 2022 introduced by President Joe Biden addressed environmental concerns and supported energy security.[9] But it also contained local content provisions which revealed an underlying motivation to favour domestic manufacturing in the US, encourage nearshoring and friendshoring of supply chains towards deeper integration in North America, and reduce the perceived 'concentrated risk'.

Under Trump 2.0, it appears that even the fig leaf of environment sensitivity has been dispensed with, and a robust and aggressive protectionist stance is the strong flavour of his Second Coming.

In the EU, German and French industrial policies include huge subsidies and protectionist 'Buy European' clauses. India's 'Atmanirbhar Bharat Abhiyan' (self-reliance campaign) and 'Vocal for Local' programmes are illustrative of the rapidly changing global economic landscape. Inherent in this new phase is the risk of deglobalization. A December 2022 Goldman Sachs report, 'The Path to 2075: Slower Global Growth, But Convergence Remains Intact', covering 104 countries, underlines that two decades of emerging markets convergence has resulted in a more equal distribution of global incomes.[10] But while income inequality between countries fell, income inequality within countries has risen. This poses a major challenge to the future of globalization.

The Economist, on the other hand, argues that we have entered the 'slowbalisation' era: World trade rose from 39 per cent of the world GDP in 1990 to 61 per cent in 2008, and fell to 58 per cent by 2019, mostly because of a slowdown in trade from emerging markets.[11] Cross-border investments and bank credit flows are down too.

A 2019 McKinsey report, 'Globalization in Transition: The Future of Trade and Value Chains', iterates that globalization is in transition from the 1990s or 2000s, which saw the expansion of complex GVCs. But production networks are not immutable; they continue to evolve. McKinsey's central finding is that GVCs have undergone major structural changes post-2009. A number of those changes house a digital technology component.

Services are playing a growing role in global value chains. Trade flows based on labour-cost arbitrage are declining in some value chains. And global value chains are becoming more knowledge-intensive.[12]

The question posed by Marcos Troyjo, former president of the New Development Bank (NDB), in 2021 is still as relevant as it was four years ago—'With so much disconnect around the world, the question today is: will deglobalisation linger or are we walking into something else?'[13] To this, we may add our own queries: What will be the defining characteristic of this different phase we are entering? Is globalization metamorphosing yet again?

First, the purchasing power and relative economic clout of various nations are changing.[14] As of end-2021, the combined GDP, measured in PPP terms, of the G7 was over 21 per cent less than that of the seven leading emerging economies, including China.

This marks a historic and historical geoeconomic shift with profound consequences for the wealth of nations and the well-being of their citizens. These consequences also relate to, as Adam Smith originally noted in his formulation of a comprehensive system of political economy, the fourth or final stage of commercial interdependence. One view is that emerging markets are increasing their commercial exchange with each other, and may offer a larger market for trade in the wake of creeping protectionism in OECD states.

The second characteristic concerns how GVCs are being rerouted by the burgeoning presence of emerging economies. This phenomenon is much broader than global supply chains as consumption will also be impacted. Geopolitics is an important driving force in reconfiguring these new value chains.

Equally, if not more, significant is the evolution of some of the world's most major economies. China, experts say, is no longer a low-cost country or a simple manufacturer of low-value-added goods; it has become one of the most important sources of FDI. It is leading the world in many state-of-the-art technologies, and accounts for an increasing share of high-technology embodied manufacturing products.

As a result, some lower-value-added economic activity has migrated from China to neighbours such as Vietnam, Indonesia, Myanmar and Bangladesh, and a trickle to India. It is a phenomenon that is not new in history—in the 1970s and 1980s, the Asian Tigers displaced Japan as low-cost, low-wage manufacturers in the region. Simultaneously, international trade and investment agreements are influencing the rerouting of GVCs. A prominent example is the Regional Comprehensive Economic Partnership (RCEP) which was signed by 15 Asia-Pacific nations in November 2020.

There is consensus among experts that in a trade system 'where the term "international" applies to the exchange of goods even at an intra-firm level', it should come as no surprise that these trade agreements influence the flows of investment. The regional consolidation of trade in the post spaghetti-bowl era holds the danger of India being left out.[15] Ambitious countries are also promoting domestic economic reforms that allow their economies to become more business-friendly, and open to FDI while being nimble about addressing core security concerns.

A case in point is China, which announced in March 2024 that it would 'further shorten the negative list for foreign investment and implement pilot programs to ease access for global companies in the fields of scientific and technological innovation [...] and broaden market access for foreign investment.'[16] The PRC has also promised to remove restrictions on foreign participation in the manufacturing sector, and continues to increase its openness in hi-tech sectors such as telecommunications and healthcare.

Its stated policy is that foreign financial entities will be granted greater access to the country's banking and insurance sectors, and the operational scope for foreign financial institutions will be expanded in China's domestic bond market as well.[17]

In parallel, the disarray in the WTO has been exemplified by the tariffs imposed on ally and adversary alike by Trump in 2025, which follow the unilateral imposition of higher tariffs on select commodity exports to China by the US in 2018, and the passing of the Carbon Border Adjustment Mechanism (CBAM) by the EU in 2022. These measures are considered to be violative of the most favoured nation (MFN) principle of the organization. The US' virtual boycott of the WTO's Dispute Settlement Body (DSB) has seriously dented the WTO's ability to oversee a rules-based multilateral trading order.

The final issue impacting globalization is talent. In this context, talent means going beyond the economic theory of comparative advantage. 'Countries need to ask themselves: What can I do besides what I am already very good at?'[18]

This is also the basis of Michael Porter's compelling argument that it is 'competitive advantage' and not the traditional comparative advantage that drives world trade flows.[19]

Countries which build their competitive advantage through the accumulation of human talent, technology, and an ecosystem supportive of enterprise have outscored others which had a comparative advantage but could not convert it to their benefit. The striking contrast between Asian economies including China and their Latin American counterparts is ample proof of this phenomenon of the supremacy of competitive advantage. India will have to learn from this contrasting experience.

To positively contribute to this metamorphosis of globalization, our focus should be on some key areas. Adherence to conventional economic models—export-led/domestic-led, public-sector-led/private-sector-led—will have to be jettisoned forthwith. For the coming decades in which the risks of a climate catastrophe are mounting exponentially, and income inequalities are becoming greater, we need a fresh approach towards people's welfare. Business as usual will simply not do.

Secondly, traditional physical infrastructure can longer be thought of as separate from the technology which enables it. New infrastructure must answer not only the needs of the twenty-first century, but also the demands of the technological transition powered by the digital revolution.

Finally, in a world where international cooperation is necessary to address the global public dangers of climate change, drug and human trafficking, and disastrous armed conflicts, providing a fresh institutional framework within which states are treated more equitably, and in sync with current realities, would help write an exemplary next chapter for globalization.

Who Will Blink First?

The ongoing fragmentation of the world economic order has occurred despite the existence of post-Second World War international institutions such as the UN with its innumerable subsidiaries, the Bretton Woods twins, and the WTO. All of them have lost credibility and, to a large extent, their effectiveness and relevance. Their domination by the Western world, led by the US, has spurred China to create a parallel universe of multilateral institutions where its voice, along with those of some other emerging economies, and not those of the West, is dominant.

The New Development Bank (NDB) and the Asian Infrastructure Investment Bank (AIIB), headquartered in Shanghai and Beijing respectively, are exemplars of this trend. BRICS, with its membership recently expanded to include capital-surplus countries, and the SCO as well as the G20 are other examples of this trend to replace post-war institutions for the management of the global order.

It cannot, however, be denied that some of these post-war

institutions did play an effective role in spreading the benefits of a multilateral framework for transferring resources to less developed economies, and a rules-based multilateral trading order across a large spectrum of nation-states. For example, ever since China joined the WTO in 2001, Sino-US trade has grown exponentially, which has benefitted both US and Chinese consumers and investors. A 2019 study by economists Xavier Jaravel and Erick Sager found that increased trade with China boosted the annual purchasing power of the average US household by $1,500 between 2000 and 2007.[20]

China is the third largest export market for the US, behind Canada and Mexico. In 2017, a study commissioned by the US-China Business Council reported that exports to China supported nearly two million jobs in the US.[21]

The notion that cross-border trade in goods should still be so widely considered the primary benchmark for international commerce, however, is robustly contested. Daniel S. Hamilton of Brookings argues that it is a completely misleading parameter in a world of extended supply chains, rapid technological change, and revived strategic competition; international commerce is more than just trade in goods—it also includes trade in services, which many pundits and policymakers tend to ignore.[22]

Services account for a smaller share of global trade than goods, but they have been growing faster. More American jobs depend on services than on goods, and services are a US competitive strength, asserts Hamilton, adding that just as trade is more than flows of goods, international commerce is more than just trade. It also includes investment—a deeper form of commercial connectivity.[23] Other flows are also critical. Cross-border data flows not only contribute more to global growth than trade in goods, they also underpin and enable virtually every other kind of cross-border flow.

The US is the world's leading hub for international trade in products delivered through data flows. International flows of research and development, and of talent, have also become critical to knowledge economies like the US. Firms now invest as much in intangible assets related to knowledge flows as in traditional capital like machinery, equipment and buildings.[24]

To understand Sino-US ties in this context, it would be useful to keep in mind that 2022 may have been the pinnacle of US-China trade, as it is now clear that both nations are trying to reduce their economic reliance on each other. While these untangling efforts are largely focused on strategic and emerging high-technology goods, the lines are increasingly blurred between what is and what is not strategic. Washington and Beijing seek to achieve this decoupling by increasing their respective domestic manufacturing capacity and capability, and diversifying import sources and export markets.

The US is embracing government subsidy policies while China continues its multi-billion-dollar effort to foster national champions. The two nations are also seeking to strengthen their respective economic and supply chain ties with countries in Southeast and South Asia, Africa and Latin America. But decoupling will take time, and de-risking will achieve only limited objectives.

We agree that the thesis playing out is that the new normal in US-China ties is one of hardening competition amid deep interdependence.[25] It is very much in the realm of probability that Washington will double down on its policy of reshoring or friendshoring, terms being used to describe US manufacturers' strategies to pivot away from China to secure supply chains either close to home, or in nations with which the US has a better relationship.

While a mass exodus out of East Asia seems unlikely for US manufacturers in the near term, with any decision to diversify supply chains away from the China-dominated region being dictated by costs as well as logistics considerations, China has, for some time, been acutely aware of the damage to its economy that such a move could cause.[26] As growth stutters in the PRC, it is attempting to rebalance its economy towards domestic demand, and shift away from exports and investment as the major drivers of growth.

The increased role of geopolitics and ideology in Beijing's economic decision-making has thus been a significant factor in its attempts to rebalance its economy towards domestic demand. Exports as a share of China's GDP peaked at 35 per cent in 2007, but fell to around 20 per cent by 2021, a level not seen since before China's accession to the WTO in 2001. Figures released in January 2023 showed that monthly exports fell by 9.9 per cent from the year before, after an 8.7 per cent contraction in November 2022. This demonstrates that net exports now make a limited contribution to Chinese GDP growth even if the recent slump in exports is attributed to Covid-19 lockdowns.[27] China's net exports hover around the $0.80 trillion mark[28] (its current account surplus amounted to $264.2 billion in 2023).[29]

One school of thought is that reducing its economic dependence on the West by creating a kind of economic fortress—the PRC's dependence on imported technology, food and fossil fuels in particular has created a substantial strategic vulnerability—is the only credible strategy for China to adopt as the Sino-US rivalry intensifies. It is certainly likely that over the next few years China will attempt to build up the country's ability to supply its own semiconductors, food and green energy sources, while in the same breath continuing to reiterate its commitment to 'expanding opening-up…to create more opportunities for the world to advance win-win cooperation...despite multiple challenges.'[30]

But this approach to economic policymaking isn't just about

China's relationship with the US and the world. Within China, too, a new emphasis on the role of the state, seemingly rooted in ideology, is increasingly apparent. In the 2017–22 period, there has been a measurable rise in the role that state-owned enterprises (SOEs) play in the Chinese economy. SOEs now account for more fixed investment in the economy than private firms for the first time since 2005.[31]

In fact, research by the Stanford Center on China's economy and institutions (January 2024) asserts that existing assessments of SOEs are flawed as most measures of state versus privately owned firms in China rely on government data from the Annual Industry Survey (AIS) to categorize firm ownership.[32]

The AIS, however, uses multiple variables to identify SOEs that, in practice, generate widespread inconsistencies in identification; its database also suffers from large-scale misreporting issues.[33] For example, firms may not change their ownership type from the initial record even after major restructuring. State ownership status is also self-reported by firms, and some of them may have incentives not to reveal their true and complete structure, making AIS records less reliable.[34]

By conventional measures, China has 391,000 SOEs. But new analysis of state ownership among all 40 million registered firms in China finds that 363,000 firms are 100 per cent state-owned, 629,000 firms are 30 per cent state-owned, and nearly 867,000 firms have at least some state-ownership component.[35] The total capital of firms with some level of state ownership had risen to roughly 68 per cent of the total capital of all firms (40 million) in the economy as early as in 2017.[36]

Whether this model means growth will suffer and China's rise will be constrained, as many expect it to be, or whether Beijing's domestic consumption, its emphasis on self-reliance based on technological innovation, and trade with non-US markets will result in adding to China's comprehensive national power, is the key unknown. What must not be elided either is that China's promotion of its BRI as an alternative model for rapid growth, infrastructure development, and employment generation has found many takers, despite the debt-trap diplomacy counternarrative offered by its adversaries.[37]

Further, the PRC's concerted pursuit of leadership in frontier technologies to pole-vault the linear growth pattern, and surpass the US, was explicitly laid out in its 14th five-year plan of 2021.[38] Beijing identified seven technology areas to focus its research on—including artificial intelligence (AI), quantum computing, and semiconductors—which is now paying dividends.[39] Robotics and biotechnology have anyway been longstanding research priorities for China.

China's 15-year-long effort to upgrade its frontier technology and R&D has enabled it to take a leadership position, even when compared to the US, in some critical green transition sectors (see chart below).

TABLE 1
Tracking Tech

TECHNOLOGY	LEAD COUNTRY	TECHNOLOGY MONOPOLY RISK
Advanced materials and manufacturing		
1. Nanoscale materials and manufacturing	China	high
2. Coatings	China	high
3. Smart materials	China	medium
4. Advanced composite materials	China	medium
5. Novel metamaterials	China	medium

TECHNOLOGY	LEAD COUNTRY	TECHNOLOGY MONOPOLY RISK
6. High-specification machining processes	China	medium
7. Advanced explosives and energetic materials	China	medium
8. Critical minerals extraction and processing	China	low
9. Advanced magnets and superconductors	China	low
10. Advanced protection	China	low
11. Continuous flow chemical synthesis	China	low
12. Additive manufacturing (incl. 3D printing)	China	low
Artificial intelligence, computing and communications		
13. Advanced radiofrequency communications (incl. 5G and 6G)	China	high
14. Advanced optical communications	China	medium
15. Artificial intelligence (AI) algorithms and hardware accelerators	China	medium
16. Distributed ledgers	China	medium
17. Advanced data analytics	China	medium
18. Machine learning (incl. neural networks and deep learning)	China	low
19. Protective cybersecurity technologies	China	low
20. High-performance computing	USA	low
21. Advanced integrated circuit design and fabrication	USA	low

TECHNOLOGY	LEAD COUNTRY	TECHNOLOGY MONOPOLY RISK
22. Natural language processing (incl. speech and text recognition and analysis)	USA	low
Energy and environment		
23. Hydrogen and ammonia for power	China	high
24. Supercapacitors	China	high
25. Electric batteries	China	high
26. Photovoltaics	China	medium
27. Nuclear waste management and recycling	China	medium
28. Directed energy technologies	China	medium
29. Biofuels	China	low
30. Nuclear energy	China	low
Quantum		
31. Quantum computing	USA	medium
32. Post-quantum cryptography	China	low
33. Quantum communicantions (incl. quantum key distribution)	China	low
34. Quantum sensors	China	low
Biotechnology, gene technology and vaccines		
35. Synthetic biology	China	high
36. Biological manufacturing	China	medium
37. Vaccines and medical countermeasures	USA	medium
Sensing, timing and navigation		
38. Photonic sensors	China	high
Defence, space, robotics and transportation		
39. Advanced aircraft engines (incl. hypersonics)	China	medium

TECHNOLOGY	LEAD COUNTRY	TECHNOLOGY MONOPOLY RISK
40. Drones, swarm and collaborative robots	China	medium
41. Small satellites	USA	low
42. Autonomous systems operation technology	China	low
43. Advanced robotics	China	low
44. Space launch systems	USA	low

Source: Australian Strategic Policy Institute[40]

This significant success in sunrise sectors is surely noteworthy. China's ageing population, however, presents considerable economic and social challenges. The decennial census released in 2021 showed China's population at 1.41 billion people, marking the slowest growth rate since the 1950s.

Over the next few years, China will lose 70 million of its workforce. This will not only impact the country's growth but also be a shock to the global supply chain which has China at its core.[41] China is ageing at a rapid pace as well; it will take just 20 years for the proportion of the elderly population to double from 10 per cent to 20 per cent (2017–37).[42]

This trend is particularly worrisome for Beijing as China's rapid growth in past decades has been tied to its demographic advantages. Policies aimed at increasing the birth rate alone are unlikely to reverse this trend. The PRC's ageing problem, together with the possibility of China being caught in the middle-income trap, though dismissed by officialdom, has ramifications for the PRC's relentless economic rise.[43]

The extent of the impact of this potential double whammy, playing out on the contours of China's economic prowess which has been the engine for the augmentation of its CNP over the past two decades, will be key to its geoeconomic competition with the US. The scenarios which could emerge as a result would need to be subjected to multi-disciplinary analyses. India will also have to factor what it learns into its own policymaking as it attempts to assert its rising power status, and negotiate the PRC's economic dominance in Asia and the Global South at large.

China is undergoing a marked slowdown in potential growth, coming down from 7.7 per cent in 2010–19 to a projected four per cent in 2024–29 and 2.5 per cent in 2030–39 according to various estimates. Most of this slowdown is driven by demographic factors. Will this lead to the collapse of the CPC's rather dystopian version of Rousseau's social contract with the Chinese people? Is it possible that economic decline—as opposed to rising incomes—will be the harbinger of a social transition in China?

Examining the institutional foundations and political reasons for China's economic growth, economist Wei Zhao provided, in 2015, what he termed a 'framework of a state-market-society triple helix for macro-level analysis.' In doing so, he underlined the point that the Chinese economic performance is reinforced and amplified by its social institutions of labour market segmenting and a unique regime of capital accumulation.[44] The so-called Chinese market economy is constructed as an ensemble of capitalists by the state, which constantly stabilizes and legitimizes the institutional arrangements.[45]

On the other hand, with its nominal GDP pegged at $27.72 trillion[46] and a GDP per capita (PPP) of $74,578,[47] the US is by far the world's largest economy, though, according to Goldman Sachs (2022), China is expected to overtake it by 2035.[48] But this is 10 years later than Goldman Sachs' 2011 projections, primarily reflecting its downward revisions to China's potential growth. Despite an optimistic prognosis, albeit pre-Trump 2.0, for the

American economy and a 'soft landing' predicted for the global economy by the IMF (January 2024 World Economic Outlook Update), sustaining economic growth and its status as the world's most prosperous nation will be a significant challenge for the US going ahead.[49]

This is not just an effect of the rise of China and other emerging economies gaining ground, but also because of American domestic issues given the political and societal polarization in that country. US efforts to emerge from the highly disruptive first Trump presidency may, it appears, come undone with the return of Donald Trump to office.

It would not have been easy for America anyway, given the geoeconomic transition that is underway, to focus on re-inventing itself, innovate, engage with the rest of the world, and attempt to reassert its global leadership position rather than seeking refuge in isolationism, which formed the basis of US economic prowess over the past 75 years. Trump 2.0 has arguably made the task that much tougher.

Global growth is projected by the IMF at 3.1 per cent in 2024 and 3.2 per cent in 2025, with the 2024 forecast being 0.2 percentage point higher than that made in the October 2023 World Economic Outlook. The higher estimate in 2024 is on account of the greater-than-expected resilience in the US and several large developing economies, as well as fiscal support for propping up economic growth in China.[50]

The IMF forecast for 2024–25 is, however, below the historical (2000–19) average of 3.8 per cent, with elevated central bank policy rates to fight inflation, a withdrawal of fiscal support amid high debt weighing on economic activity, and low underlying productivity growth. Inflation is falling faster than expected in most regions, in the midst of unwinding supply-side issues and restrictive monetary policy. Global headline inflation is expected to fall to 5.8 per cent in 2024 and to 4.4 per cent in 2025, with the 2025 forecast revised down.[51]

The world should not require the IMF to underscore the fact that if deep multilateral coordination is not prioritized, debt resolution, avoiding debt distress, creating space for necessary investments, and mitigating the effects of climate change will be non-starters. There is a message here for both Washington and Beijing if surviving in the same international economic system, or what remains of it, is to be a reality going forward. The alternative is more of what we are witnessing currently as the pace of the splintering of the world economy picks up, and nations are forced to choose sides.

The current state of the global order is 'less union' and 'more disunion', as the commentator Andrew Sheng put it. One indicator for this is the price of gold rising over $2,222 per troy ounce in 2024 (and hitting an all-time high in 2025). A higher gold price means a weaker dollar in real terms.[52] Before the US markets dipped as a result of Trump 2.0 policies in the first few months of 2025, the Dow, S&P 500 and Nasdaq stock market indicators had touched record highs in the first quarter of calendar year 2024: the total market cap of US stocks increased by $10.2 trillion in 2023.[53] In the fourth quarter of 2023, the US economy grew at an above-trend pace of 3.2 per cent per year, he added.

Sheng's conclusion was that the world's largest economy had been growing faster relative to the global economy, but that was sustained by growing fiscal and trade deficits—US net debt to the world was at $18 trillion while the rest of the world was languishing. If the US spending and debt spree continues apace over the next four years, will the rest of the world continue to fund (in effect) its largest debtor?[54] And what about India? Some commentators are already cautioning Delhi against supporting the Trump way of tackling excess US consumption.[55]

The US dollar has risen a stunning 30 per cent over the past decade, yet the end-April 2024 meetings of the IMF and World Bank were the most dollar-bullish in a very long time.[56] The focus in Washington was on the cyclical outperformance of the American economy, with geopolitical developments seen as adding to the dollar's strength as the risks posed by them were not 'systemic'.[57] So putting more money into the dollar, as underlined previously, is the default option for the world as there is currently no viable alternative to it. This could be changing, though, with Trump back in the White House.

Trump seems intent on weakening the US dollar as both he and Vice-President J.D. Vance consider a strong dollar as a tax on US domestic manufacturers and a subsidy for import consumption. Reflecting this stance, the dollar weakened against the ten competing currencies' basket by over 5.7 per cent between January and March 2025. And the scenario going forward is a further weakening of the dollar as the Trump 2.0 administration plans to impose a tax on countries that buy US treasuries, in a bid to dampen the demand.[58]

The signs are that China will not be able to revert to the high growth rates of previous decades given that the US is now actively aiming to constrain its economic prowess, while Beijing is simultaneously pausing to address domestic structural issues including the real estate meltdown.

Japan, meanwhile, would likely try to normalize interest rates so that the real income for the ageing Japanese workforce may recover after years of stagnant nominal wages and a declining yen. If, on top of that, oil prices continue to remain flat at around current prices, West Asian oil producers will not have additional export income or savings as they need to invest in changing the job structure away from oil and gas industries.

Additionally, as Washington doubles down on defence expenditure, the debate around the MIC and its role in buttressing

US economic prowess has been reignited. That the American MIC is at the core of existing manufacturing in that country and its economic benefits bring immense geostrategic advantages into play for Washington are undeniable. There is economic logic behind such an assessment. According to a 2017 estimate, approximately 10 per cent of the $2.2 trillion in factory output in the US went into the production of weapons sold mainly to the defence department for use by the US armed forces and exported to other countries.[59] This figure is thought to have grown significantly since then; the MIC accounts for a big chunk of the total US manufacturing industry. The US defence market size is estimated at $617.29 billion for 2024, and it is expected to reach $651.16 billion by 2032, growing at a CAGR of 0.67 per cent, a recent Mordor Intelligence report iterates.[60]

In 2002, the combined total revenues of Lockheed Martin, Northrop Grumman and Boeing were estimated to account for one per cent of US GDP.[61] While RTX has since replaced Boeing in the top three, it's an all-American podium finish. The Aviation Industry Corporation of China (AVIC) Ltd moved up to take fourth place in 2023, pushing Boeing to fifth, but that still leaves us with four of the world's five top defence companies by revenue being US-owned.

This is not to suggest that the US has reached the war-economy stage of the post-Pearl Harbor attack period when the American domestic manufacturing capacity built in the aftermath of the Great Depression was converted to the war effort, and played a significant role in pulling the US economy out of the Depression. But it is important to draw attention to the fact that it is no longer the stuff of conspiracy theories to suggest that the MIC's role in the US economy, and the significant influence it wields in Washington policy circles, could become a critical input into executive decision-making.

Which sector of the domestic economy the US chooses to focus on, therefore, especially with a view to generating employment while meeting security challenges, is the key going forward. In the post-1945 period, the US built on its manufacturing prowess and technological strengths showcased during the hostilities to emerge as an economic behemoth from 1950 onwards.

The US was outward-looking, active in establishing institutions to regulate world trade, and the leading voice in rule-making for a single global economic system. Today, a return to isolationism and protectionism has already been initiated in the US.[62] The highly polarized domestic economic, social and political discourse in America does not allow us to be sanguine. One of the most dangerous deficits the US faces, it is argued, is not one of trade, values or military capabilities, but a deficit in understanding how it is connected to other societies around the world.[63] The political, economic and media errors resulting from this deficit can shortchange American consumers, producers, workers, and their families.[64]

In this construct, expecting the US to remain the sole engine of global recovery in the medium term is not realistic, and China's ability to take advantage of this situation is somewhat limited. This opens up opportunities for other intermediate powers to leverage the geoeconomic transition to their advantage. India's position must be to ensure its competitive advantage by exercising a laser-like focus on globally comparable infrastructure, building talent that is also world-quality, and growing its R&D footprint.

India and the Rise of a Trading Bloc

Understanding how the global trade landscape is shifting will help Indian policymakers prepare for globalization's next chapter and the opportunities and challenges it will present. The future of trade is intermediate services, says economist Richard Baldwin, and this is good news for workers in emerging markets.[65] That the nature of trade has fundamentally changed—and is changing—is not in doubt. What Baldwin and others are saying is that the future of global trade will be in digital services, not physical goods. And that despite deepening geopolitical fault lines, most countries understand that preserving ESG-compliant trade for SMEs would help create domestic jobs.

The establishment of standards, processes, and clearing and payment systems for the changing trade landscape is critical, and nations that have skin in the rule-making game are likely to be the winners. Sluggish global trade growth is symptomatic of rising protectionism and the risk of deglobalization. Globalization, though, may not be faltering, but instead transitioning from the 1990s and 2000s that saw the expansion of complex value chains across the globe.

Simultaneously, as India is not a part of any of the three mega trading blocs, it makes it more difficult for the country to successfully compete with peers like Vietnam and Bangladesh.[66] This policy needs to be reviewed, and concerted follow-up measures undertaken, to improve competitiveness across all sectors of the economy. Thus, policy design which incorporates a cross-sectional perspective and identifies our priorities, rather than merely asserting our needs, is essential.

Indian policymaking is currently largely reliant on bilateral arrangements to enhance trade, judging from the spate of free trade agreements (FTAs) signed and under negotiation. For instance, India's recent FTA with the EFTA bloc of countries comprising Switzerland, Norway, Iceland and Liechtenstein is being celebrated for its focus on sustainable development, transparent procedures, and fostering a favourable environment for trade and investment in line with India's commitment to inclusive growth.[67] Indeed, the inking of this agreement is an exemplar of India's proactive approach towards bilateral trade agreements, and marked its fourth FTA in three years since 2021, following agreements with Mauritius, the UAE and Australia.

These came, significantly, after a 10-year hiatus, during which even bilateral agreements were avoided on the grounds that those already in place like with Sri Lanka, South Korea and Thailand did not promote India's exports. Negotiations for FTAs with the UK, EU and Oman are also ongoing, which could add to India's expanding trade partnerships.

As in multilateral or regional trade blocs, however, benefits from bilateral FTAs accrue only and only if the country has ensured that its firms achieve the required productivity levels which make them globally competitive. The push for expanding manufacturing capacities under the production-linked incentive (PLI) framework is a necessary and desirable step in this direction. But except for the electronics sector, which has been a runaway success with exports (led by the smartphone surge) worth $22.5 billion in the first eight months of FY 2025,[68] the jury is still out on the 12 other sectors which are covered under the PLI scheme.

The dogged pursuit of FTAs could also prove of some utility for India to push back against China's assertive presence in multilateral trade platforms such as the WTO. The WTO's 13th Ministerial Conference (MC13) in 2024 witnessed Beijing press hard for the International Facilitation Agreement, which met with dissent from several nations due to its contentious clauses.

In this milieu, cultivating bilateral economic and trade ties, including expediting negotiations over FTAs, offers India the opportunity to forge deeper political connections with nations other than the Big Two, and expand its geoeconomic influence in a targeted manner. But will these be enough to navigate global trade dynamics? Can FTAs replace or at least be a substantial palliative for India not joining the RCEP or an approximate arrangement?

We are simpatico with the argument that having opted out of the RCEP and being ineligible for USMCA/EU membership, India should consider establishing a fourth trading bloc with African and West Asian economies given the ongoing transition of economic heft from OECD countries to the nations of the Global South. The logic behind the argument is that the momentum of economic growth, which is both sustainable and inclusive, will now inevitably shift to the Indian Ocean Rim with an extension into sub-Saharan Africa (SSA), and even further into coastal North or Northeast Africa. That this is a rising economic region, given its vast reserves of critical minerals and a demographic structure that will remain robust even beyond 2060 when India starts ageing, is also beyond doubt.

But given the variables in play, especially in terms of extant or potential armed conflicts, as well as a deteriorating security situation and unstable societal conditions, we hesitate to make an emphatic recommendation.

India would, however, do well to focus its attention on developing deeper and wider economic ties with this region, and achieving greater economic integration based on its own strengths. Expanding trade ties with African and West Asian economies is important even if it does not necessarily translate into the creation of a fourth mega-regional trade bloc. To achieve this expansion, India will have to, first and foremost, put in a massive effort to ramp up its share in the import of goods and services of these countries.

A beginning can be made by the Indian foreign policy establishment encouraging the Indian Foreign Service (IFS) cadre to prioritize expertise on the region as a preferred career choice.[69] Given India's aspiration to play a more substantive role on the global stage, the size of the Ministry of External Affairs (MEA) also needs expanding. Despite some expansion in recent years,[70] the Indian diplomatic cadre needs further strengthening with a larger number of domain, sector and regional specialists being inducted, rather than merely upping the intake of career diplomats.[71]

There is also a need for changing the focus of the foreign affairs establishment from 'political relations' to achieving greater economic benefit for the Indian corporate sector. Facilitating technology transfers to Indian firms, attracting foreign direct investment (as opposed to foreign portfolio investment), and promoting Indian exports in every country should now be the basis of the performance evaluation of Indian diplomats stationed abroad.

External Affairs Minister S. Jaishankar has said that formulating a foreign policy for a *viksit* or developed economy for a post-Nehruvian nation and a globalized world is the task India has set itself.[72] The implication is that a strongly growing, globally interconnected economy is its *raison d'etre*.

It is, therefore, only rational for our missions abroad to be focusing principally on accelerating India's economic growth. In this regard, a proposal once under consideration by the government to co-opt officers of the Indian Economic Services into the IFS cadre deserves another look. Personnel from these services can serve as economic and commercial counsellors in our missions, and help re-orient the focus to securing economic advantage for India in bilateral ties.[73] There is also a strong case for India's economy-related ministries and foreign office to focus equally or more on the IOR and SSA, as compared to the attention lavished on OECD countries. Given the multiple simultaneous global transitions underway, it is understandable if Delhi wants to move thoughtfully in this matter. However, setting a clear direction would be useful, nay essential.

Finally, as many global corporations and multinational companies revamp their GVCs and transition to a China+1 strategy to diversify their country risk, emerging economies such as Vietnam have successfully created an enabling ecosystem, for example in the electronics sector, to attract and retain GVCs. For India, treading firmly on the GVC path is not just advisable, it is also a necessary condition for sustainable growth. The question, however, of what comes first—making a place in GVCs, or privileging domestic value addition (DVA)—needs urgent resolution. Also, developing a regulatory and policy architecture that facilitates the development of auxiliary indigenous industries which supply raw materials and intermediate inputs to lead firms must be a priority.

Integrating into GVCs has the potential to overcome the challenge of jobless growth in India, and result in a more inclusive economy. While this would also align with the vision of SDG 8 (promoting inclusive and sustainable economic growth, employment and decent work for all), batting for DVA will need to be proceeded with very cautiously as a premature push could boomerang.

To sum up, the world is seemingly headed towards a multipolarity that will take concrete shape over the next two decades during which the Chinese economy will surpass the US in size as Europe tries to retain its share in the global economy.[74] Europe will likely attempt to prevent the emergence of a 'messy duopoly' between the US and China, but may have to accept it if its internal dynamic deteriorates. Either of these alternatives yields the unsavoury prospect of India being left out and on its own.

For India to successfully navigate its future trajectory through the unfolding geoeconomic transition, it must engage with all or both sides in a multipolar or bipolar world to varying degrees.

But its focus has to be on achieving rapid and sustainable economic growth upon which everything else hinges. The direction and intensity of the transition in the coming decades will be determined majorly by the nature of engagement between the world's two largest economies, i.e. China and the US.

Given its civilizational history and strengths, India has an opportunity to carve out a key role—perhaps in cooperation with both Africa with its young population and vast mineral resources, and South and Southeast Asia which is home to a vast pool of talented human resources and shares millennial ties with India, that is Bharat.

The following possible scenarios emanating from the geoeconomic transition would, therefore, merit the attention of Indian policymakers:

(i) Will the competition between the US and China drift towards open economic confrontation riddled with rising protectionism and the snapping of economic and financial flows between them? Technology flows are already hugely impeded, and the two countries are pursuing their independent trajectories.

(ii) US-China rivalry will most likely result in a greater fragmentation of the global economy. How does India then take advantage of global markets and the external demand to sustain its rapid economic growth? We will need to re-imagine our EXIM policies, and focus on increasing our share in selected sectors of the global markets.

(iii) Could America and China, already deeply integrated, agree to a duopoly? Such a scenario will likely see a long period of hegemonic contestation for economic supremacy. It may result in the global economy being divided into regional blocs, and force a choice on India to join one of the blocs. How do we prepare for this eventuality?

(iv) China may yet falter and get caught in the middle-income trap because of its unfavourable demographics. Though unlikely, China's possible stumble could yield not only lessons for us to avoid the middle-income trap but also an opportunity to become the second largest economy in the world behind the US. But China will surely not accept such an outcome sanguinely.

(v) Can we work together with Africa to help it recognize its potential and look for global examples to emulate for the continent's own multiple transitions?

(vi) The fact that the climate window is closing at a faster rate implies higher costs of development, making SDG targets unfeasible. Whither India?

The issues listed above will surely also be shaped by the equally transformative transitions in the five other domains identified. The cumulative impact of the six global transitions will thus have to be factored in to formulate an appropriate policy response that will allow India to achieve its aspirational goals.

Bringing these multiple and differentiated aspects together is indeed a herculean task. The central thesis that we propound in this book is that there is no way to avoid the massive effort required to shape the simultaneous transitions to our benefit. And that we as a people can succeed in doing so given the necessary leadership which has the courage to think boldly for solutions rooted in India's ground realities.

FOUR

SHIFTING CLOUT

OECD to Global South Transition

In 2020, the World Economic Forum (WEF) published an important paper on the 'new gold' of our times, viz. data, vast quantities of which have been yielded by digitalization.[1] The nations of the Global South have this new gold in abundance. Hitherto, member-states of the Organisation for Economic Co-operation and Development (OECD) comprising the developed economies had mostly possessed the technologies and capacities to mine this data, which offers opportunities for business, human well-being and the environment.

The rise of China, which has access to both data and technology, started changing all that with new business models generating top-line value. Other emerging economies of the Global South too are now navigating in that direction. India has the additional advantage—as a democracy premised on rule of law—of being able simultaneously to preserve individual agency and privacy. Innovations to advance and refine this new paradigm for 'the business of data' are a key component and accompany the transition of economic power away from the OECD countries to the emerging markets of the Global South.[2]

The purchasing power and relative economic heft of nations are changing. This shifting clout is reflected in the fact that even by 2019, the G7 had a combined GDP, measured in purchasing power parity (PPP) terms, of $40 trillion, while the Emerging Seven (E7) economies of Brazil, China, India, Indonesia, Mexico, Turkey and Russia had inched ahead with a combined GDP in PPP terms of $53 trillion.[3]

Non-OECD economies are expected to account for 57 per cent of GDP by 2030 as the economic influence of the G7 states shifts to the E7 bloc; by 2040, E7 economies are forecast to be double that of the G7.[4]

In another example, the combined GDP of the expanded BRICS-plus coalition of countries in 2025 crossed $31 trillion.[5] The RCEP with a nominal GDP of $26 trillion and a population of 2.27 billion in 2020,[6] meanwhile, is a bigger trade bloc than the EU (GDP $15.38 trillion,[7] population 447.69 million[8] for the same year). India, though, is not a part of the RCEP.

Even the pandemic-induced slump in Southeast Asian exports seems to be well and truly over, with recent numbers (July 2024) showing ASEAN economies, including Thailand and Malaysia, logging their fastest growth in two years in July. This rebound is largely driven by renewed overseas demand for electronics, in line with the upswing in the global semiconductor cycle.[9] Intra-ASEAN exports, which account for over 20 per cent of the total for the regional bloc, too have picked up. The days of the G7 economies calling the shots on the direction and pace of global economic growth seem to be behind us. Emerging markets are also increasing their commercial exchange with each other and may offer a larger market for trade for each other.

The transition of economic heft from the OECD to the Global South can be traced to the now advanced, industrialized economies of East Asia (Japan, South Korea, Taiwan) providing the initial momentum in the second half of the twentieth century, the Latin American economies beginning to perform (before succumbing to the middle-income trap), and the Southeast Asian economies then getting going.

Nevertheless, over the second half of the past 50–60 years, it is unquestionably China which has been the standout contributor in providing the GDP spurt for Asia, while the oil-rich West Asian economies have contributed significantly to the growth in GDP per capita.[10] India's growth story too has made some advances over the past two decades. Just the two Asian giants account for 36 per cent of the world's population and 25 per cent of global GDP.[11]

China and India will be responsible for a rising share of global output as the world's economic centre of gravity continues to shift toward the Global South, especially Asia. China's GDP will likely surpass that of the US by 2035, while India's GDP could do so by 2075.[12] The individual purchasing power of OECD countries' citizens, though, is likely to remain higher than that of consumers in China and India.

Therein lies the rub. The economic dominance of the West may be ending but it's unlikely to be replaced in the same measure. Veteran Singaporean diplomat Kishore Mahbubani argues that the fora and institutions of the Global South are gaining heft nonetheless. He points to the humble origins of the BRICS forum, which started life in 2009 derided in some quarters as less of a counterpoint to the G7 and more of a marketing gimmick. Today, BRICS is an exemplar of the shift of economic power: In 1980, the G7 accounted for 50 per cent of the world's GDP in PPP terms, while the BRICS countries—excluding Russia, then part of the Soviet Union—accounted for 11 per cent.

Today, the G7 accounts for 30 per cent of the world's GDP which is on a par with BRICS' share of the global GDP.[13] The Global South is also home to a large majority of the world's population and is projected to experience significant demographic expansion in the coming decades. By 2030, 4.8 billion people will be middle class. Two-third of this globalized, more affluent community that will possess significant purchasing power will reside in the Asia-Pacific region.[14]

The writing is on the wall. For instance, the EU's share of global trade has fallen by one-third to second place (16 per cent of global trade in 2021), compared with China (28.3 per cent) and the US (14.5 per cent) since 2001—thanks in large part to a significant technology component.[15] The European Round Table for Industry (ERT) [EU Competitiveness and Industry] Benchmarking Report 2024 indicates how the continent is racing against the clock as European industry has been continuously losing ground in global markets in terms of market share; EU companies are becoming less relevant and Europe's future technological leadership is at risk.[16, 17]

Research and development (R&D) in, and application of, advanced and emerging technologies are only hastening the economic transition to the Global South. Europe's adoption of 5G technology, for example, is way behind that of China or the US. The related and real issue is: Who drives the structural changes? In the US, the corporate sector remains dynamic and committed to profits and innovation. In China, the party/government takes the lead, permitting corporate competition that is aligned with national goals, iterates an incisive commentary.[18] While Europe is in imminent risk of getting marginalized because of its refusal to undertake structural reforms, there's still fight left in the US, and China continues to rise despite hiccups. The lessons for India from these trends are critical.

By 2050, according to PwC, the E7 markets could grow twice as fast as advanced economies (G7) on average; six of the seven largest economies in the world would be emerging economies led by China (first), India (second) and Indonesia (fourth); the US could be down to third place in the global GDP rankings, while the EU27's share of world GDP could fall below 10 per cent by 2050; the UK could be down to tenth place, France out of the top 10, and Italy out of the top 20 as they are overtaken by faster-growing emerging economies like Mexico, Turkey and Vietnam, respectively.[19]

While the implications of this ongoing economic transition for India and other emerging economies will be profound, and are yet to fully play out, for any forecasts to come to fruition, emerging economies like India need to enhance their institutions and their infrastructure significantly if they are to realize their long-term growth potential.

Intrinsic to the economic transition away from OECD member-states to the nations of the Global South has been the resurgence of Asia over the past fifty years. Significantly, Asia's economic rise has been on the back of various countries in the continent following heterodox paths for their rejuvenation.

The East Asian Tigers adopted an export-promotion strategy instead of the then fashionable import-substitution strategy, to witness a miraculous economic transformation in the 1960s. Thereafter, during the 1980s, other Asian economies adopted a pragmatic piecemeal approach instead of the shock therapy advocated by the prevalent neo-liberal thinking to make a transition from planned economies to market economies, redefining the relationship between governments and markets.[20]

Professor Deepak Nayyar, while charting the story of the continent's development over half a century (1968–2018), writes that Asia's economic transformation in just fifty years—which is a short time span in history—has been remarkable. Asia's growing engagement with the world economy has been an integral part of that process, while the dramatic increase in its relative importance for the world economy is an outcome of that process.[21] Asia's growing economic significance in the world between 1970 and 2016 is illustrated by the fact that its GDP rose from 8.7 per cent of the world economy to 29.9 per cent over that period.[22]

The economic transition from OECD countries to the nations of the Global South is, of course, not limited to Asia. Equally, it could not have occurred without Asia. And the central narrative of this transition is China's unprecedented growth.

The New China Playbook

The consequences of China having more or less reclaimed its economic might of the 1800s are readily discernible in its attempts to create a parallel universe of multilateral institutions to challenge the US-led world economic order.

The New Development Bank (also known as the BRICS Development Bank) and the Asian Infrastructure Investment Bank (AIIB), headquartered in Shanghai and Beijing respectively, are attempts to establish equally well-resourced financial institutions like the Bretton Woods twins and their regional clones. The inclusion of capital-surplus Asian countries like Saudi Arabia, Iran and the United Arab Emirates (UAE) in BRICS will surely give greater heft to the BRICS Bank and make it a significant competitor to the Washington-based institutions.

Asia's ascendancy is also manifested in Chinese investment in the Asia-Pacific region, which rose sharply in 2023. Chinese investment totalled nearly $20 billion across the Asia-Pacific, up 37 per cent, led by Indonesia.[23] It also logged about $17 billion in construction contracts, partly financed by Chinese loans, marking a roughly 14 per cent increase from 2022.[24]

China is seemingly in pole position to influence the so-called Global South's trajectory: first, by utilizing diverse state instrumentalities including the Belt and Road Initiative (BRI) in developing countries and strategic partners, particularly in Asia; secondly, through its mercantile but effective policies in developing countries, especially in Africa and in the Indian Ocean Region; and thirdly, by leveraging its economic heft-enabled strategic foreign policy as was seen in the Saudi Arabia-Iran detente brokered by

President Xi in 2023, as well as the derecognition of Taiwan by Kiribati and the Solomon Islands a few years earlier.

As it is unlikely that the shift of economic power from the OECD countries to non-OECD ones will be accompanied by a simultaneous replacement of the Western norms-based international economic order, we can expect each country to look out for itself. It's safe to predict intensifying chaos as a result, where even minimal adherence by nations to collective norms will be a cause for celebration.

Analysts simpatico to Beijing's worldview are pushing the narrative that for emerging and developing economies navigating a turbulent world of intense geopolitical rivalry and worsening climate warming, the question of a new development model is top of the growth agenda.[25] For many nations of the Global South, this is an attractive position, as they are currently under pressure to choose sides between the US-led affluent West and a BRICS grouping with growing economic heft that seeks an alternative order to the current G7-dominated international economic system—especially when the free-market order is in retreat in many parts of the globe as tariffs and sanctions are raised unilaterally, with industrial policy and state intervention rising by the day.[26]

The Big Fat Indian Engagement

As the transition of economic power to the Global South intensifies, there is little clarity on the international economic governance mechanisms which may emerge. A central question, however, emerges: Is India's external economic engagement model coming full circle, to the 'good old days' of the South Commission et al.? Well, not quite. Because relying excessively on bilateral cooperation, trade and technology-transfer agreements may be a sub-optimal policy response for India to negotiate the transition. But policymakers of a certain vintage may be forgiven for evoking a creeping sense of déjà vu.

For, while India's twenty-first century relationship with—and putative leadership of—the Global South does imply a renewed focus on recalibrating its relations with other developing countries, the focus is now clearly on economic interaction, especially relating to greater connectivity, trade and the flow of capital without the distraction of what could be termed (today) an irrelevant ideological dimension.

The geostrategic flux and heightened uncertainty of the global economic order in the three decades after the end of the Cold War suggest that deepening mutually profitable South-South economic engagement has acquired criticality for India. A relationship which, to deploy a cliché, privileges trade over aid and investments over loans portends a much longer-lasting arrangement.

This stands in contrast to one premised on the construct of post-colonial nations' solidarity, which greatly exaggerated the convergence of developing countries' interests. This is not to say that there should not be a humanitarian and/or soft power dimension to the relationships India must re(build) in the Global South, but to underline that ideological affinity cannot be the basis for India to leverage the ongoing transition.

It is not about being transactional but ensuring a win-win situation wherein developing nations are incentivized to work together. Indeed, the Global South perspective on geoeconomics recognizes that states may pursue economic policies not just to enhance their own economic well-being, but also to build partnerships that can reshape global governance structures.

India's need for infusion of capital, transfer of technology, and expertise sharing from the advanced nations of the Global North to achieve its development objectives, however, cannot be ignored. But the perception, especially in the developed world, that India is underwhelming as an investment destination is not one that can be altered in a hurry.

Delhi cannot escape responsibility for this perception taking root. In spite of the efforts of successive governments in the post-liberalization era, lack of progress on the reform of labour and land laws, the persistence of systemic rent-seeking despite initiatives aimed at reducing the compliance burden and promoting ease of doing business, poor and uneven law-and-order enforcement, and judicial atrophy are just some of the pain points for investors from rich, capital-surplus countries. Yet, engaging the Global North economically in the short to medium term must not be ignored even as India intensifies its economic engagement with EMs across geographies. And Delhi seems to have twigged, judging from the plethora of FTAs either signed and/or under negotiation with rich countries.

Whether the FTA model is the optimal way to go for India vis-à-vis the Global South, however, remains an open question. Not only because the objective conditions are distinct, but also because as the OECD-Global South transition acquires pace, many of the countries India wants to do more business with have already signed up to the RCEP and/or have otherwise been subsumed into China's supply chains. Beijing's leadership of the Global South is only growing stronger despite the narrative highlighting the danger of debt diplomacy for developing nations.

It is an unpopular thought to air, but perhaps finding a way to work with China instead of against it is the best course for India to follow to leverage the economic rise of the Global South. For example, India could actively encourage Chinese FDI in all non-security-sensitive sectors—yes, we know, 'everything is strategic' but that's a zero-sum game and Delhi has to take a calculated risk to grow rapidly. In return, India could get China to relax non-tariff barriers, which, at present, restrain Indian exports from entering Chinese markets.

If Beijing agrees to also ease the path for Delhi to join the RCEP by assuaging its concerns, all of Asia's developing nations would benefit. Indeed, the Global South including China, India, ASEAN and the GCC acting in concert on major continental issues could change the game in Asia.

It is a prospect that would enable the nations of the Global South to meet the several major challenges of climate change and job creation in the face of AI/robotization, and to address stark inequalities and the demographic transition.

Chinese scholar Zhang Jie notes India's significant efforts in recent years to strengthen its leadership status among countries in the Global South via multilateral organizations, summits, economic assistance initiatives, technology sharing, scholarship programmes, and exports of digital infrastructure.[27] (Of particular note are the bilateral defence agreements India has concluded with Vietnam, Egypt and Argentina, apart from its amplified soft-power projection.)

However, underlining the Chinese party-state's perspective, he locates these Indian efforts in the framework of Sino-US economic and security competition, asserting that Delhi is seeking leadership of the Global South to compete with China for economic and political influence and in the process, deepening ties with a Washington that is looking to isolate China.[28] For this reason, in Zhang's view, most developing countries are lukewarm to Indian overtures.

Indian policymakers know they forget at their peril that the Global South's emergence as a critical actor in international affairs is closely linked to its growing economic weight. These countries account for over 40 per cent of the world GDP, 23 per cent of global merchandise trade, and over 65 per cent of inward foreign direct investments (FDI), with major economies like China, India and Brazil driving this growth.[29]

Joining the Battle in Earnest

By dominating the Global South in economic terms, the Chinese will, over time, also dominate it in political terms. India would then be in danger of being left with the crumbs of the Global South leadership. The way out, therefore, is to tread the hard yards required to position ourselves along with China as the twin economic engine of the developing world, albeit in a *ceteris paribus* setting.

As *The Economist* puts it, Chinese firms in industries from cars to clothing have expanded abroad with startling speed. A new commercial contest has begun. Its battleground is neither China nor the rich world, but the fast-growing economies of the Global South.[30] India needs to join the battle in earnest.

Delhi has made a start by affirming South-South cooperation as a modality of cooperation in which nations of the Global South establish horizontal partnerships for the sharing of knowledge, training, technology and expertise in order to facilitate development.[31] Such a construct is guided by principles going back to the 1970s, including respect for national sovereignty, non-conditionality, non-interference in domestic affairs, and demand-driven mutual benefit.

The 11 areas of potential action identified by the UN Secretary-General provide an indicative though not exhaustive list of issues to pick from.[32] There is, though, genuine frustration among developing countries like India with the inability of the multilateral framework to address key developmental challenges for nations of the Global South.

The credibility of the main UN body mandated to promote South-South cooperation, United Nations Conference on Trade and Development (UNCTAD), is severely damaged. The unit for Economic Cooperation and Integration among Developing Countries (ECIDC), housed in UNCTAD, was set up in 2010 as a research body to inform policy, support South-led governance efforts in the multilateral system, and contribute to technical cooperation. It has had very mixed results, to put it gently.

There is a plethora of other organizations and fora working on getting the Global South going: United Nations Office for South-South Cooperation (UNOSSC), South-South Galaxy, hosted by UNOSSC, which is a global knowledge-sharing and partnership-brokering platform, South-South Global Thinkers, the global coalition of think tank networks from the Global North and Global South supported by UNDP and UNOSSC, the South Centre, an intergovernmental organization of developing countries that helps them to combine their efforts and expertise to promote their common interests in the international arena, and the Alliance of NGOs and CSOs for South-South Cooperation (ANCSSC), which too works with the UNOSSC.

All very impressive on paper, but there isn't too much to show for their labours. India would do well not to invest too much time and effort here. There are also other, left-field developments, which India needs to factor into its policy design to manage the transition. The primary among them is the dollar's status as world reserve currency, which provides the US a unique ability to use the payment system to achieve national objectives besides economic growth. The US has increasingly relied on the payment system to achieve non-economic objectives, mostly but not exclusively in the foreign policy domain.

The ramifications of increased reliance on the payment system for the projection of US foreign policy—and China's attempts to forge a Global South alliance that backs the development of an alternative payment system—could exponentially hasten the transition of economic heft to the Global South. India's efforts to engage the Global South through the Voice of the Global South Summit (VOGSS) align well with PM Modi's underlining of our commitment to global welfare as a *Vishwa Bandhu* (global friend) while eschewing any hints at unwelcome patronage.[33]

But while India's positioning is on-spot, its performance in terms of robust mutual trade and investment for the nations of the Global South is as yet sub-par. The Chinese undermining of Indian efforts is not helping, of course. But there may be a sliver of opportunity for both countries to shape the economic potential of the Global South in a less tendentious, win-win-win manner.

If India and China can implement the consensus reached by PM Modi and President Xi at their meeting during the October 2024 BRICS summit in Kazan, Russia, hinted the Chinese Foreign Minister Wang Yi at the G20 meeting in Rio de Janeiro in November of the same year, it will be in line with the 'fundamental interests of the two peoples, the expectations of Global South countries, and the right direction of history.'[34] That's as close as one gets to the CCP version of an olive branch.[35]

A Sliver of Opportunity

Against the backdrop of the geoeconomic shift and China's significant lead over India in GDP terms—five times larger—and in cutting-edge technology, Delhi faces a strategic choice. It is, on balance, likely to be better off cooperating and working with Beijing in the Asia-Pacific region, in particular, rather than competing with China for the leadership of the Global South at this stage. That day, too, will hopefully come.

We are, in any case, *de facto* working with China in fora like BRICS, SCO, G-20, and the BASIC bloc (collaborating to combat climate change), and are members of the BRICS Bank and AIIF. In essence, we have all the pre-conditions even for *de jure* cooperation. The test case or first objective for a putative Sino-Indian compact could be the willingness of both countries to work together to assuage Indian concerns and clear Chinese doubts to ease the path for India joining the RCEP on terms both Beijing and Delhi can live with.

Collaborating with China to further strengthen BRICS in its expanded form and initiate the framework for establishing a new set of relevant global institutions to replace those set up by the US-led West after the Second World War is perhaps inevitable. Such an effort will be in sync with the ongoing shift in the geoeconomics—which in our view is likely to intensify rather than be rolled back, Trump or no Trump.

The bottom line is that it is in India's interest to seek an independent and critical role in the emerging multipolar world order and, indeed, to prevent a global duopoly from becoming a *fait accompli* in which our strategic autonomy will, by definition, be severely limited. The transition of economic heft from the OECD to the Global South provides India an opportunity for growing rapidly and enhancing its international standing. Provided our policies are nuanced right.

FIVE

THE GOLDEN MEAN

Technological Transition

The technological transition, along with the transition away from carbon, is perhaps the most disruptive of the six simultaneously unfolding global transitions. Given the vast scope and myriad aspects of the transition, we have focused the chapter sharply on the following:

(i) Outlining the generalized framework for making advanced technologies more effective efficiency-boosters while preventing further environmental degradation and without widening inequalities in Indian society
(ii) Enumerating the measures to address the multiple challenges that are bound to emerge as new technologies get adopted and assimilated in production and distribution networks
(iii) Discussing the philosophical underpinnings of the technology regulation imperative and the urgency for adoption of frontier technologies by India to pole-vault the traditional, linear growth path
(iv) Analysing the geopolitics of technology and suggesting strategies to negotiate it
(v) Reflecting on the state of global governance of frontier technologies and the path forward for India

Changeling, Gamechanger

The world, India included, is in the midst of the sixth technology revolution. And like the five preceding it, the ongoing revolution, comprising essentially of Internet 2.0 and artificial intelligence (AI), promises to be even more transformative than earlier ones. It is undoubtedly ushering in a new era in humanity's evolution.

A powerful energy is being released by the rapid proliferation of advanced and emerging technologies which the world is currently experiencing. These technologies cut across the economic, societal, political, cultural and psycho-social domains. Their impact will soon be as ubiquitous as that of electricity.

The five earlier technology revolutions were:

(i) Steam, which replaced human and animal motive power and which could be harnessed in ever-increasing scale
(ii) Electricity, which created a 24-hour working day, allowing energy transmission over long distances for universal access
(iii) Mass manufacturing that achieved unprecedented scales of production and forced workers to conform to the rhythm of the assembly line, producing standardized products that were not susceptible to human error or fancies
(iv) The internal combustion engine (ICE), including the aero version, which dramatically reduced travel time and effectively shrunk global geographies to make the world into potentially a single marketplace
(v) The advent of the World Wide Web (WWW) or the internet with its potential for eliminating information asymmetries, making communication instantaneous across immeasurable distances and creating the basis for the Internet of Things (IoT) that made machine-to-machine interface possible without human intervention

The internet had already demonstrated its potential to replace the routine mental work that humans perform. Now, in its open-source, digitally empowered *avatar*, Internet 2.0, which is at the core of the ongoing sixth technology revolution, is replacing complex mental operations like medical diagnostics, legal counselling, influencing consumer behaviour, transportation, and remotely controlled warfare.

It surely also has huge potential to ramp up labour productivity and achieve superior and faster outcomes. However, it also has the capacity to completely replace human effort across the widest range of sectors, operations and processes. Robotics have quickly replaced workers on the assembly lines, as bank tellers, and in a large number of hazardous operations across the entire economy. The question, as always with technology transitions, is whether states or societies can harness its positive features for improving the welfare levels of the population. Or will the negative features be allowed to dominate the outcomes, resulting in unsustainable inequalities across countries and within each economy?

The latter will be the outcome if the 'haves' corner preferential access to new technologies and enhance their productivity while the 'have-nots', who lack the needed financial resources and skills to harness new technologies, see their productivity levels and living standards stagnate or even slip below existing levels as their functions are replaced by technology-driven substitutes.

The technology transition has its staunch opponents and proponents. Historical evidence is strongly supportive of the understanding—adopted in this chapter—that technological progress is inevitable and cannot be stopped in its tracks. Only when technology posits an existential threat, global consensus emerges to restrain further progress in a particular direction. The sole unambiguous example of this thus far has been the global accord to stop further work on cloning technology when Dolly the Sheep became the first cloned mammal in 1996 and caused a sensation when she was presented before the world's media the next year in the UK.[1]

Apart from cloning, nuclear warfare technology has also seen a degree of global convergence on restraining further accumulation of destructive power—but this came about only after the world stocked enough weapons to ensure mutually assured destruction several times over. Certain other tech advances in the security realm, undertaken secretly, still go on. The fact is that the security-defence sector has historically been the exception to the notion of 'Technology as a Global Good'. Universalism in this respect doesn't work in the global commons. The capabilities afforded by advanced and emerging technologies to states in relation to armed conflict, deterrence and surveillance make them innately much more consequential than technology breakthroughs of previous eras.

What, then, ought to be our philosophical approach in dealing with the technological transition? That evolving an ethical framework is critical to managing a phenomenon which holds the potential to upend millennia-old patterns of human existence is, to our mind, inarguable. We offer no comment on the technologies themselves and/or their applications—that's best left to the domain experts—but confine ourselves to suggesting certain principles for further discussion.

A section of critical voices including that of Professor Noam Chomsky see the use of generative (gen) AI and ChatGPT-style systems, among other emerging technologies, as 'basically high-tech plagiarism' and 'a way of avoiding learning'. Gen AI, Chomsky has famously and provocatively stated, may have some value for something but it's not obvious what.[2]

We frame the issue somewhat differently:

- Is it (a) desirable and (b) possible to separate and prioritize the *application* of advanced technologies into notional categories, each with its own customized regulatory architecture?

- Is domestic and international consensus on the rules of the game possible?
- What are the processes to be followed by means of which affixing human responsibility at the beginning of the digital chain for the information generated by big-data-based statistical programmes in human-intelligible mode can be achieved? Gen AI, for example, may be an aggregator of data at unprecedented scale which it then disseminates in human-intelligible language form, and structure; but what of the accuracy and factual basis of the data itself?
- How will the copyright and intellectual property rights of content generated with the help of advanced technologies be accounted for?

We are clear that the twin operating principles applicable to an orderly and meritocratic regulation of the entire gamut of human-machine interactions are that of an oversight architecture and human accountability. For this to be brought to fruition, a well-defined use of the legitimate instrumentalities of the Weberian bureaucratic state to regulate human activity is essential. Indeed, French political philosopher Montesquieu's separation of powers principle (*The Spirit of Laws*, 1748) could well be applied to tackle the technology transition.

As a first step, even the possibility of human-origin responsibility being elided on the basis of the dangerous claim that a technology/programme could, in a manner of speaking, develop a life of its own, needs to be negated. For, it stands to reason that the humans (modelers) behind the programmes being used by other humans (consumers) must be held accountable.

The recognition of the requirement to set acceptable ethical and normative standards for AI is universally accepted.[3] The onus is on India to ensure it is an integral part of international consensus-building so that our priorities are integrated into any global agreement on the development and direction of advanced technologies.

No Longer Science Fiction

The global urge to restrain further AI advances has been triggered by the imminent possibility of sentient AI that could threaten societal cohesion and the ability of the human race to chart its own destiny.[4] The UN Secretary-General's Special Envoy for Digital and Emerging Technologies highlights that traditional governance approaches fall short of addressing the rapid development of AI technologies. There is a need to update these global governance tools to ensure accountability and bridge the gap between the private sector and regulators to develop a 'shared understanding' of the consequences and benefits of AI.[5]

Towards this goal, there have been three international conferences in the recent past with the agenda for determining global governance norms for AI—starting with the Bletchley Park AI Safety Summit in 2023, followed by the UN Global AI Resolution of March 2024 and the AI Seoul Summit of May 2024. Each of these conferences was targeted precisely at achieving global convergence on the nature and direction of future developments in AI in sectors. In business, for instance, this can be better understood by looking at the role of trade secrets in the business landscape.

A trade secret is defined as information that has actual or potential economic value from not being generally known to or readily ascertainable by others, and the owner of which takes reasonable measures to keep it secret. AI systems raise a new set of questions regarding trade secrets because they can generate economically valuable information that was not originally in the possession of their human designers. Suppose, asks technology and law Professor John Villasenor, that an AI system develops a trade secret that no person is aware of. Can this information qualify as a trade secret, despite no human knowing about it?[6] It is in such contexts that a state-initiated, independent experts-populated and monitored regulatory structure complete with compliance burden—which may appear disincentivizing to tech laissez-faire proponents—is necessary. But great care must be taken to ensure its design does not stifle innovation.

The fear of humungous statistical programmes run on predictive algorithms replacing critical human thinking at some point in the future which has permeated popular discourse—the Man versus Machine idea—also merits a mention. For, the airing of such apprehensions is no longer susceptible to being dismissed as the irrational fears of neo-Luddites. As Madhumita Murgia writes in her recent book *Code Dependent*,[7] AI can strip away our collective and individual sense of agency, and shatter our illusion of free will. The so-called Godfather of AI, Geoffrey Hinton, underlined in a series of interviews, in Spring 2024, the existentialist threat to the human race posed by digital intelligence, which he himself had helped create.[8]

'I no longer believe it is science fiction,' he iterated.[9] Hinton has asserted in his public interventions that we have to start thinking about how to control the fallout of these fast-progressing advanced technologies 'now, not 20 years later'.[10] A sense of urgency needs to be imbued in this effort as multimodal chatbots are arguably already having subjective experiences.

Such concerns have prompted researchers and thought leaders to advocate for a concerted effort to 'reclaim our humanity', warning of advanced tech's potential to change what it means to be human. Preparing to manage extreme AI risks—including large-scale social harms, malicious uses, and an irreversible loss of human control over autonomous systems—is a complex task. This requires not just technical research and development, but also adaptive, proactive governance. Equally, those arguing for caution and not alacrity in embracing advanced technologies would do well to fully recognize the transformative benefits to humankind the technology transition could provide.

We suspect this dilemma between 'AI doomers and AI accelerationists'[11] has arisen from a conflation between: (a) domains where advanced technologies and their applications require urgent adoption and deployment for inclusive, rapid green growth, and (b) domains where there's a compelling argument to monitor their seductive ability to inveigle themselves into all spheres of our existence and potentially morph into a sinister challenge for the autonomous existence of humankind itself. How to go about unmixing the above is best left to domain specialists mapping the development of technologies and those elected for ensuring citizens' well-being. This cohort may perhaps be guided in their effort by Jeremy Bentham's fundamental axiom suitably paraphrased: To envisage the greatest happiness (and benefit) for the greatest number, that is the measure of right and wrong.[12]

These words ring even truer given the findings of a recent study which suggest that AI does not boost base capabilities equally—performance improvement in lower-skilled professionals increased by about 43 per cent but for highly-skilled professionals the boost was only 17 per cent, which would suggest a 'jagged technological frontier'.[13] Also, the adoption of frontier technologies will not impact all countries equally. And in some domains such as education, the need for creating an India-specific framework to manage AI implementation is essential as it is going to be a major disruptor. UNESCO has already created detailed frameworks for AI implementation in education.[14]

The need to evolve a broad consensus at the centre of the

technological transition debate is thus ever more pressing; policy is not made at the fringes.

Missing Pieces in India's AI Puzzle

The emerging global convergence on limits to AI will not, however, stop or even restrain further advances in Industry 4.0 with its fulcrum on human-machine interface (HCI) and boosting efficiency in a sustainable manner. India must harness Industry 4.0 as quickly and as comprehensively as it can. Only then will the country be able to meet the enormous challenge of achieving exponential economic growth while simultaneously reducing its carbon footprint and reducing inequality across its provinces and population segments. Successfully harnessing Industry 4.0 and the sixth technology revolution on which it is based will enable India to leapfrog over several stages of its economic growth trajectory with sustainability and greater equity. India simply cannot afford to miss this bus.

It is imperative for India to focus on how it can take advantage of frontier and emerging technologies like AI, but also others in material science, quantum computing, and biotechnology, for instance to achieve its goal of exponential, sustainable and inclusive growth.

Our principal focus is on measures that can be taken by the government and the corporate sector, preferably together, to more effectively harness these frontier technologies in as short a time as possible. At the same time, attention has also to be directed to prevent the negative impact of these technologies from becoming dominant and overshadowing their positive impacts.

India faces the complex challenge of successfully tackling the technology transition vis-à-vis its national priorities: rapid, equitable and green economic growth; achieving OECD-comparable HDIs for its citizens; minimizing our technology vulnerability; putting in place a robust security architecture; and enhancing our CNP.

In the short or actually the immediate term, India needs to ensure that it can firmly maintain its sustainable, inclusive and rapid growth trajectory. In the medium to long term, our approach towards the technology transition will have to be directed towards our security imperatives of reducing technology dependence and building our CNP to the desired levels.

Our argument is that the two sets of priorities, viz. accelerating economic growth and building a robust technological capability that contributes to our CNP, require a differentiated approach towards tackling the technology transition.

Short-Term Measures

The short-term priority, in its starkest form, is for the Indian firms acquiring, adopting and adapting frontline technologies to attain global competitiveness across the spectrum of sectors in which they operate.

This is the *sine qua non* for accelerating our economic growth. The key performance indicator (KPI) for Indian firms having successfully harnessed frontier technologies could be the well-established criterion of a rising share of Indian firms in global production and world trade flows in the sectors in which they choose to operate.

The importance of putting in place and using such a criterion cannot be overemphasised. A very large number of technology missions and initiatives come a cropper in real terms because of the absence of such a KPI. With this criterion in place, several subsequent measures can be taken to facilitate firms to acquire, adopt and adapt frontier technologies at all stages of the supply chain, including marketing and branding in these sectors.

First, Indian firms should be free to choose the nature and source of frontier technology needed to make them globally competitive. Policy should indeed make it more attractive for these firms to work together with domestic science and technology (S&T) entities in developing technologies that are superior to those available from external sources. Imported technologies come with very high royalty and licence payments and often with restrictions on access to external markets.[15]

Firms will choose to work with domestic science and technology institutions if their upfront costs of commissioning the required R&D is lower than the net present value of intellectual property (IP) payment flows over a finite number of years. Policy intervention could help lower these upfront costs and encourage the adoption of indigenously generated technologies. But a strict caveat is in order. Domestic firms would always be free to choose between the external and domestically developed alternatives and not be forced to choose the domestic option because they have received some fiscal, technical or policy support from the government.[16]

Secondly, technology scanning is a critical requirement of successful technology acquisition by domestic firms, which require as much information as possible on sunrise technologies for upgrading their production capacities. Technology scanning across global horizons thus becomes a critical activity, which can be profitably undertaken by a third party dedicated to this function. Indian companies can then be directed to the sources of such technologies for acquiring the IP commercially or through joint ventures with foreign companies which have the IP.

This was presumably the basis of setting up the Technology Information, Forecasting and Assessment Council (TIFAC) within the Department of Science and Technology (DST) in 1988.

Rajiv Kumar recalls several conversations with Dr Y.S. Rajan, the first executive director of TIFAC, who was clear that the mandate for TIFAC was to scan the global technology scene and prepare a roster of technologies which would be of interest either to domestic firms or to various laboratories under the Council of Scientific & Industrial Research (CSIR) network. These emerging technologies would then be acquired and developed further to create their indigenous versions.

Over the years, however, as visible from its website, TIFAC has apparently abandoned its scanning and forecasting activities and now focuses more on nurturing start-ups, surveying domestic technology developments, and supporting small and medium firms' absorption of technologies identified by the firms themselves. It is important to resurrect TIFAC's technology scanning, forecasting and assessment mandate.

In our view, the most effective and expeditious way forward would be to set up an autonomous entity on the same model as National Payment Corporation of India (NPCI), which oversees the most successful UPI payment system, or the Digi Yatra Foundation (DYF) that has revolutionized the security system across Indian airports, or indeed the Open Network for Digital Commerce (ONDC), a unique Indian effort to challenge the dominance of large retail corporations that monopolize markets through vast network externalities, giving them massive scale economies.

The two central features of these three successful entities are:

- First, they are established outside the government and are managed as autonomous non-profit entities which have clearly stated objectives and time-bound KPIs for performance evaluation.
- Second, all three entities have used the most advanced versions of digital technologies based on Internet 2.0 to successfully build digital public infrastructure (DPI). Several countries are now wanting to emulate this achievement.

TIFAC could be converted into a similar non-government, non-profit, autonomously managed entity with an oversight board comprising senior officials from the science and technology establishment, academia and the private sector. The board's responsibility will be to establish the KPIs for TIFAC and then monitor performance to achieve accountability.

Thirdly, government procurement remains a critical component for successful technology upgradation by existing or new firms. The US and China are the best examples of the hugely important role that government procurement can play in encouraging domestic firms to acquire and operate new technologies that may not yet have been proven to be commercially viable.

Several Chinese companies, which today dominate global markets in their sectors, started on the basis of large-scale and persistent preferential procurement by the government in their earlier stages. In the US, the entire military-industrial complex (MIC) that now dominates the world markets has come up as a result of close ties between the private sector and the government, which adopted preferential procurement. In Japan, the practice of *amakudari* (descent from heaven), by which senior state officials after the end of their tenures in government are parachuted into large Japanese corporations, ensures that Japanese firms benefit from preferential procurement by the government.

In India, some price preference, of about 15 per cent, is given to domestic firms in government tenders for both goods and services. Most often, however, other tender conditions, like the experience requirement or scale of output already achieved prior to bidding for the particular tender, rules out participation by domestic companies, especially start-ups.

Fledgling private entrepreneurs need active and persistent government support through preferential procurement for them to take the risk of acquiring or developing new technologies, especially those whose commercial viability is not yet proven. Some progress has been made by the government in this regard, specifically in the procurement of defence equipment and supplies.

In 2013–14, the expenditure in respect of orders placed to foreign vendors for capital acquisitions was Rs 35,082 crore.[17] The Modi government first showed its commitment to bringing down this dependence through a progressively introduced system of reserving procurement contracts till a certain value for domestic suppliers. It has now decided that any import of defence equipment/sourcing from a foreign entity, irrespective of value and type of acquisition, should only be an exception requiring the specific approval of Defence Acquisition Council (DAC)/Defence Minister.[18] The expenditure on defence procurement from foreign sources has reduced from 46 per cent of the overall expenditure in 2018–19 to 36.7 per cent by 2022, according to government data.[19] Further, a record 75 per cent (approximately Rs 1 lakh crore) of the defence capital procurement budget was earmarked for domestic industry in financial year 2023–24, up from 68 per cent in 2022–23.[20] There is, however, still much scope for effectively using government procurement for successful technology upgradation across the entire spectrum of sectors in India.

Fourthly, ease of doing business (EoDB) is a necessary condition for successful technology transition. Firms upgrading their technology and moving into frontier technology spaces face substantial risks as well as elevated uncertainty levels. They need the maximum stability in their operating environment and minimal regulatory and compliance burden. The optimal model is for public sector agencies to take care of all basic and routine activities like land acquisition, provision of utilities and regulatory compliances.

Several countries have successfully established industrial enclaves where firms are free from all such routine functions and can focus their attention on adopting and adapting new technologies to achieve global competitiveness. There have been similar efforts in India but a great majority of these have not succeeded in attracting and nurturing frontier technology enterprises. Effective EoDB will be achieved only through collaborative working between the government and private enterprise.

The government's role has to change from that of a heavy-handed regulator to becoming an active supporter of private enterprise, with the objective of reducing the uncertainty that entrepreneurs have to face while negotiating the technological transition.

Over the last ten years, the government has initiated several programmes to provide EoDB for start-ups, including technology start-ups. The Champions of Change initiative, managed by NITI Aayog, was an attempt by Prime Minister Modi to sensitize central government line ministries to the constraints being faced by such start-ups. The Startup India initiative, launched in January 2016 under the Department for Promotion of Industry and Internal Trade (DPIIT), also has a similar mandate.

Its 19-point action plan is aimed at building enhanced infrastructure; facilitating IPR acquisition; providing necessary financing from the Rs 10,000 crore Fund of Funds (FFS) managed by Small Industries Development Bank of India (SIDBI); and enabling access to a network of entrepreneurs which can be accessed for cooperation and guidance for resolving constraints. It will be critical to regularly monitor the progress of Startup India and other similar programmes of the central government. The most important input for its success will be the active and positive role of state governments. It is at the state level and indeed at the district level that young entrepreneurs trying to make a breakthrough interface with the government's regulatory and administrative system. The DPIIT will do well to establish a robust monitoring system to track the progress of all start-ups and work with state governments to address the EoDB issues faced by companies attempting to upgrade their technologies.

Medium-Term Measures

In the medium to long term, the objective has to be to enhance India's capacity for generating frontier technology.

First, an important systemic requirement for making the optimum use of frontier technologies would be to actively promote a synergistic collaboration between all the science and technology institutes irrespective of them being in the public or private corporate sector. In several Indian cities such as Delhi, Bengaluru, Pune and Hyderabad, there are more than 40 public sector science and technology institutes operating presently in silos, with negligible interaction among their faculty and researchers.

Given the multi-disciplinary nature of frontier technologies, a beginning can be made by encouraging all these public sector science and technology institutions in any one city to work together on collaborative projects and share resources. In fact, a committee headed by the Vice Chairman of NITI Aayog—and comprising the Principal Scientific Adviser to the Government of India and other senior experts—recommended the establishment of a city-based network of these institutions led by a CEO who would be responsible for encouraging systemic collaboration among the institutes. But it will take a substantial policy push and a well-crafted set of incentives for active project-based collaborations among these premier S&T institutes.

Secondly, a serious effort has to be made for encouraging greater collaboration between public and private sector R&D establishments. Some progress has been made in recent years with the setting up of Centres of Excellence for selected technologies.[21] These centres bring together representatives from academia and experts in the CSIR labs. Private industry, however, has still held back from joining these collaborative initiatives. The importance of such collaboration has long been recognized but success in achieving it has been elusive. There might well be some systemic issues which need to be identified and addressed for greater public-private collaboration.

Thirdly, greater interface between defence-oriented R&D, conducted primarily in institutions under the Defence Research and Development Organisation (DRDO), and civilian R&D units, including those in the CSIR network, would also come within the purview of fostering partnerships for technology upgradation.

The focus of all these efforts will be to generate maximum synergies within the S&T establishments operating within the country. This will help in negotiating the technology transition more effectively.

Fourthly, there are a very large number of science and technology experts of Indian origin working in universities and advanced S&T institutions in developed countries. This diaspora represents a vital pool of human capital that could help India tackle its technology transition.

There are several schemes already in place under the CSIR rubric to try and attract such talent to Indian institutions.[22] But evidently these have not yielded the desired results so far and need to be reviewed and revamped. We can learn from the Koreans and the Chinese in this respect as both these countries have been noticeably successful in attracting S&T experts back from foreign universities and labs. A more flexible and open-minded stance has to be adopted for achieving the desired results.

Fifthly, the most important issue in successfully managing the technology transition is to raise the R&D spend in the country. The total R&D expenditure in India in 2023 was reported to be 0.64 per cent of GDP. This compares very unfavourably with 5.7 per cent in Israel, 2.41 per cent in China, 4.8 per cent in Korea and 3.47 per cent in the US.[23] India's sub-$100 billion spend on R&D in 2024 was 'dwarfed' by China's annual spending at roughly $496 billion,[24] while the US' was estimated to have been well over

$900 billion in 2023.[25] Critically, the private sector's share in total R&D spend in India is only 36.4 per cent as compared to 71 per cent in China and 75 per cent in the US.[26]

This low level of R&D spending in India by its private corporate sector is reflected in the near absence of product innovation during the past seven decades of the evolution of S&T system in the country. The key question facing us today is how to convert India into an economy that promotes, nurtures and rewards product innovation. The scale of national R&D effort and its quality has to be transformed. Otherwise, India faces the prospect of dangerously lagging behind other major economies and not benefiting from the ongoing technology transition.

The government has taken cognizance of this challenge. It initiated the Atal Innovation Mission (AIM) in NITI Aayog in 2016 with the explicit objective of establishing incubation centres to nurture innovative start-ups and set up Tinkering Labs in secondary schools. During 2016–21, more than 70 incubation centres and 10,000 Tinkering Labs were established.

While these are commendable initiatives to encourage innovation and enhance students' practical exposure to new tech applications, they are not a substitute for the urgent need for ramping up fundamental and high-quality R&D in the private corporate sector, which alone will take India into the front ranks of technologically dynamic economies.

It is vital that a systemic approach, one that synergizes public and private R&D efforts, is designed and adopted for converting India into a 'product nation' and enabling it to optimize the adoption of emerging technologies.

A major initiative in this regard has been launched by the Indian Software Product Industry Round Table ('iSPIRT'), the organization of tech-volunteers principally responsible for putting in place, over the past few years, the globally recognized DPI in

India. Experts postulate that DPI has the potential to reach 50 countries (and not just of the Global South) in a few years.[27]

The DPI today has several components, which together constitute the India Stack. It comprises digital financial interface and digital health data; Digi Yatra that uses facial recognition for secure travel; and DigiLocker that provides all necessary identification in a secure manner for citizens. The iSPIRT model is based on a dynamic partnership between non-profit and non-government entities and the government establishments.

This model can be effectively extended to achieve successful outcomes in other carefully selected sectors, termed as winning bets by iSPIRT, in which India would like to reach global technology frontiers. The model needs to be detailed and a convergence reached between concerned government agencies and selected non-government actors to push forward the R&D agenda in the chosen sectors. The effort will be even more successful if the private sector could also be brought in as a partner in pursuing these technology bets in which India aims to pole-vault to the global cutting-edge in the selected technology.

The necessary condition for this is the building of trust between all three stakeholders: the government, non-profit actors, and the corporate sector. To achieve this trust-based cooperation and convergence, the government will have to yield its leadership position to the non-profit entity and support its efforts in a mission mode to successfully achieve the technology bets. This may also propel the private sector to increase its R&D spend as it will be assured of a higher return on its investment once the bets are successful.

It is quite clear that large private corporations in India have a larger outlay on their government relations departments compared to their outlays on R&D. The reason surely is that the perceived rate of return on addressing government regulations/

compliances is higher than on R&D. This perceived reality can be changed only by dramatically reducing the regulatory and compliance burden for all private enterprises.[28] Even more than large corporations, the reduction in the regulatory burden will benefit technology start-ups and small and medium enterprises (SMEs) which do not have the wherewithal to invest in setting up large government relations departments.

Finally, it merits repetition that product innovation is the key to making our economy globally competitive and for Indian companies to garner a larger share of world markets in sectors in which they operate. For successful product innovation, some choices or bets will be necessary. These, when successful, yield enormous returns in terms of higher price realization and a greater share in global markets.

The probability of bets being successful becomes qualitatively higher if the selection of these bets and the operational strategy to make them successful is premised on trust-based and convergent partnership between the government, private enterprises and non-profit civil society organizations.

The Bhashini app, for example, shows great promise in overcoming the linguistic diversity problem and also the difficulty people have in reading long written forms. It can be a great equalizer.

The platform enables text-to-text translation in 22 Scheduled Indian languages and offers automated speech recognition, text-to-speech synthesis, optical character recognition, video translation, document translation, and language detection. It also provides financial services such as voice-based payments.[29]

The adoption of advanced technologies by India could help move the country from the lower end of the manufacturing technology spectrum to the more complex products which require advanced design capabilities and sophisticated manufacturing systems. But the technology transition has to be midwifed with extreme care to avoid unmanageable disruptions at scale.

Globally, protests are growing against the massive job losses caused by the adoption of technology, especially in the logistics sector. Longshoremen at docks along the US East and Gulf coasts, for instance, went on strike in September–October 2024 for the first time since 1977 as trades union took a hardline stance against automation, which is spreading rapidly in ports the world over.[30]

How long before their Indian counterparts—aided and abetted by political parties across the board which recognize that job losses are a surefire way to lose elections—follow suit, is anybody's guess. Our estimate—not very long. Especially as being acutely sensitive to socio-economic upheavals is, in a sense, part of a political organization's KRA.

Therefore, a massive effort will be required to retrain and reskill our young workforce to ensure that the large-scale adoption of frontier technologies does not exacerbate the inequalities in our society by disrupting employment potential and economic growth both in the services and the manufacturing sectors. To be orderly and in sync with societal needs, the technology transition will have to be premised on the domestic legislative, regulatory and operational ecosystem that the government can put in place once we have consensually identified our national priorities.

Geopolitics of Technology

Enhancing India's global technological heft is not going to be easy. Doubling down on R&D spends, providing a policy push for collaborative public-private efforts, and promoting innovation for the development of tech applications are, of course, necessary. But technology transfer and deep collaboration with leading technology companies and countries must also be on the table for India. An interdisciplinary assessment is, therefore, critical to understanding the geopolitics of the technological transition including its implications for India's economy and its national security. As a tech maven put it: Balance of Innovation is the key to Balance of Power.[31]

For a start, the widely used nomenclature of 'AI Nations' to refer to those states with some advanced tech capacity, while it makes for ease of communication, is somewhat misleading. Globally, states with access to advanced tech are far too heterogenous in terms of capacity to be clubbed together in a single category. To begin with, Delhi will have to deal with both the US, the established tech superpower, as well as China, which has already overtaken the US in 57 of 64 critical technology areas, to augment its own tech capabilities.[32]

The US has been notoriously stingy when it comes to tech transfer and collaboration with India despite some so-called marquee deals. The most prominent of them has been the General Electric (GE) Aerospace-Hindustan Aeronautics Limited (HAL) MoU of June 2023 under which the former agreed to transfer 80 per cent of the technology (up from 58 per cent when negotiations first began in 2012) to produce fighter jet engines for the Indian Air Force.[33]

The view in a section of the Indian policy establishment appears to be that in the long run, as it were, the reaffirmation of the Indo-US Comprehensive Global Strategic Partnership in February 2025, including the launch of the COMPACT (Catalyzing Opportunities for Military Partnership, Accelerated Commerce & Technology) and TRUST (Transforming the Relationship Utilizing Strategic Technology) initiatives, lays the ground for deeper, more meaningful bilateral ties which will help India tackle the tech transition more optimally.[34] Delhi, it must be assumed though, is surely not unaware of the strings which come attached.[35]

China, on the other hand, clearly envisions its place in a changing geopolitical environment based on growing its strategic space. If in the process the PRC exhibits and/or can be persuaded to exhibit greater flexibility in sharing advanced and emerging technologies with India, Delhi definitely needs to keep its options open. This is not to argue that there will be no strings attached by the Chinese, but to emphasise the fundamental point, accelerated and economical technology transfers have to be prioritized on a source-agnostic basis by India.

In the global landscape, the US and China are the technological superpowers, followed by a handful of second-tier states, and a larger group of tier-three states with limited access to advanced technologies. And then comes the vast global advanced-technology underclass.

But there's also the view that there's a stateless dimension to the geopolitics which is evolving, and the digital domain is accelerating it.[36] While this is perhaps an accurate forward-looking assessment, it is unlikely to be the dominant factor in the tech transition for the near future given the pushback by countries across the globe to ensure the primacy of the nation-state in the international order.

The reality is that it's the no-holds-barred China-US competition to develop critical technologies that is producing second- and third-order effects across geographies. Beijing, it appears, is in the process of establishing a monopoly in some areas, and leads in fields such as electric batteries, hypersonics, and advanced radio-frequency communications like 5G and 6G. Quantum computing, space launch systems and vaccines are among the seven critical technology fields in which the US still has the edge. While China and the US are by far the leaders in advanced technologies, a small group of states led by the UK, Europe, Japan and India are beginning to make a mark in some areas.

Both the US and China, however, are benefiting disproportionately from a clustering effect around technology hubs. Of the approximately 4,500 AI-involved companies in the world, about half operate in the US and one-third operate in China.[37] According to a widely cited study by PricewaterhouseCoopers (PwC), the US and China alone are set to capture 70 per cent of the $15.7 trillion windfall that AI is expected to yield to the global economy by 2030.[38]

India can hope to bag a seat at the high table of global governance of technology and emerge as a rule-maker instead of a rule-taker only if it invests wisely and massively in advanced and emerging technologies. For that to come to pass, growing our indigenous tech base and promoting innovation is vital. But it is technology transfer and deep-tech collaboration with the domain leaders which will be key to this effort in the immediate future.

The question then becomes a quintessentially geopolitical one: Which of the two superpowers will India benefit from in a collaborative technological partnership, and what is the pay-off Delhi is willing to live with? (Pacts with other intermediate AI nations such as the UK, Netherlands, France, Japan and South Korea would be useful but not necessarily transformative even if we can fill in the data gap for, say, Japan or South Korea, which may have the prowess to build advanced-tech-powered economies of scale but lack the data.)

Semiconductors: New Battleground for Great Power Competition

Examining sensitive semiconductor chip-making technology is educative in this context. It powers the digital revolution and has become a significant part of the new battleground for great power competition. Semiconductors, it is now clear, will play a crucial role in global geopolitics, much like the role that reserves of oil and gas have played thus far. McKinsey & Company estimates that the global semiconductor industry will be a $1 trillion industry by 2030.[39]

The supply chain disruptions due to COVID-19 made the world realize that currently China and Taiwan dominate the value chains of the semiconductor industry, giving a thrust to the 'China-plus-one' strategy.[40] Hard power in its economic and military dimensions is today built on a foundation of computer chips.

China, on its part, is pouring billions into chip-building initiatives. The Americans have, meanwhile, leaned on their allies, most prominently South Korea, Taiwan, Japan and Netherlands, to try and slow down Chinese technological and military advances by strengthening semiconductor export controls and shaping supply chains.

The US' global dominance had hitherto stemmed from its ability to harness computing power more effectively than anyone else. This is now under threat. While Washington has had its way, there is acute discomfort in Seoul and even in Tokyo and within Europe at the economic damage from following the US diktat vis-à-vis China.

China has protested vigorously, asserting that such moves will damage not only its domestic semiconductor industry but also the global economy, and will be detrimental to the 'long-term interests of consumers worldwide'.[41] Beijing is also attempting to circumvent the obstacles placed in its path by further strengthening its high-quality research institutes.

But it is China's inroads into Africa to secure its supply chain of critical minerals and rare earth elements (REE) that have been the gamechanger. The US-Ukraine critical minerals and rare earths deal and the US coveting Greenland need to be seen in this context, as the US attempts to make up lost ground.[42]

Rare earths are essential components that go into the production of electronics (computers, televisions and smartphones), renewable energy technology (wind turbines, solar panels and electric vehicle batteries), and defence equipment (jet engines, missile guidance/defence systems, satellites, GPS equipment, etc.).

Some African states, encouraged by the US and EU in part, have also started pushing back against China's 'predatory practices' in the rare earths mining sector.[43] The Chinese, however, have pivoted quickly and moved into Central Asia—Kazakhstan in particular and even Afghanistan—to develop alternative access to critical minerals deposits.

The technology transfer landscape is, therefore, a critical area of engagement for India. Deep collaboration with the technology superpowers could provide us access to advanced and emerging technologies as well as augment our domestic research abilities. Also, the integration of these technologies into our national security priorities will hasten the opening up of politico-military options for Delhi, and provide us an opportunity to leverage the international situation to our advantage over the next decade.

Security Realism

The advantages of being an early adopter of technological progress are historically evident. And the critical and transformative importance of new technologies cannot be understated for India. Sans a robust regulatory architecture, however, there is a danger that the technology transition may end up undermining rather than helping create a knowledge society.

Intricately related to the discussion on the geopolitics of technology is the impact of the technological transition on national security and the military capability of states. The unfolding consequences of this transition have the potential to affect a fundamental shift in the global balance of power.

Outlining a detailed strategy to deal with this phenomenon would need another volume, but a few pointers are warranted. It is no longer possible to ascertain what is strategic and what is not, especially in the security sphere. From cyber to space, equity markets to semiconductors, and social media (dis)information strategies—advanced technology has smuggled itself into all domains in plain sight. Security realism is the key going forward as the technological transition gathers pace. For, it would be naïve to believe that nations with the wherewithal to augment their military capabilities would not do so or enter into sensitive technology transfer deals with any but a few strategic, pact allies. In fact, attempts are being made to restrict technology knowhow with military applications even to close allies by both US and China.

That the major technology powers will attempt to set the pace and promote international governing structures for advanced and emerging technology applications to their benefit in the military-security domains, should be considered as a given. Great powers are thus pursuing the objectives of enhancing national defences using advanced technologies, shaping the international cyber environment by leveraging technological and economic capabilities, and defining international tech norms. The template for this approach already exists in the UNSC P-5 getting the rest of the world to sign the Nuclear Non-Proliferation Treaty (NPT) (bar major outliers India and Israel), while retaining their own nukes, leading to charges of 'nuclear apartheid'.

But the world is a very different place today from the second half of the twentieth century, with the rise of China and the increasing global heft of the Intermediate Powers. As our discussion on the geopolitical and geoeconomic transitions highlighted, the emerging multipolar world order with aspects of a messy duopoly reflected in it opens up options for India.

The deep impact of the technology transition is also apparent in the new, advanced-tech-driven revolution in military affairs (RMA), defined as a fundamental change in the nature of warfare. The rapid development of advanced technologies is making the cyber, space and deep-sea domains key theatres of contestation, deterrence and conflict. The military capabilities of major powers are increasingly attuned to these themes and underline the need for a source-agnostic tech transfer regime for India.

While the global community has begun to engage and negotiate the rules for the future development of advanced technologies, it is already being accepted that national security establishments of all countries will continue their R&D to secure their citizens from all manner of threats, internal and external. A wide range of emerging technologies have military applications—including cyber technology, AI, and quantum technology.

The extent of their incorporation into the Indian armed forces will prove critical over the coming years. As Michael O'Hanlon writes in his well-regarded monograph *Security, Strategy, and Order: Forecasting Change in Military Technology: 2020-2040*, technology is advancing fast in many realms but it is not enough to wave one's arms exuberantly about futuristic military possibilities. The stakes are too high. Defence resource decisions need to be based on concrete analysis that breaks down the categories of major military technological invention and innovation one by one, and then examines each, he writes, adding that areas where things are changing fastest may warrant the most investment as well as the most deliberation on how to modify tactics and operational plans to exploit new opportunities (and mitigate new vulnerabilities that adversaries may develop as a result of these same likely advances).

For India, private sector participation in developing applied technologies for the armed forces and internal security organizations is urgently needed and can be mutually profitable provided trust can be built. Another challenge India needs to overcome is slow networks, which are vital for a range of activities including intelligence gathering and real-time dissemination at the bottom of the security pyramid. Finally, it must be underlined that the weaponization of information and the spread of disinformation are critical to subjugating an adversary's population without the use of force. Tech advancements like gen AI and deep fakes have only aided and abetted the use of these tactics by India's adversaries, both state and non-state.

There is no getting away from the central issue: The global rivalry for leadership is not just about military or financial power, but about having the technological edge and its ability to continue to generate wealth. That has its own consequences.

Golden Mean Redux

The global technological transition is shaping economies and societies. The pace at which advanced technologies are evolving makes their unfolding impact not just an important but also a highly unpredictable driver for India's—and the world's—future trajectory. They could, on the one hand, put millions of jobs at risk almost overnight, and the downstream effects of adopting such technologies without essential due diligence and putting appropriate guardrails in place can cause unprecedented disruption of the existing socio-economic order. On the other hand, the danger of the baby getting thrown out with the bathwater is ever present, and one which must be guarded against. Because we know that technological progress is inexorable and overall beneficial.

For India, in particular, deploying advanced technologies optimally and strategically can create a potent mix of resources and infrastructure that can yield more equitable and more sustainable growth. Unlike developed countries, most of the developing world has a large young population—India, for instance, has a median age of just 29. Advanced technologies offer a huge opportunity to raise labour productivity, build a knowledge society, enhance our demographic dividend, and make the 'youth bulge' employable and thereby productive.

Once an expert-led, national priorities premised, and real-time reviewable regulatory structure is in place to govern the application of advanced and emerging technologies, a hundred flowers—with no apologies to Mao—ought to be encouraged to bloom within it. But the 'move fast and break things' strategy is rather risky, to put it mildly, for the future of humanity. It may also not be the best way to tackle an unprecedented technological transition.

There are some ideas which may be developed on the regulatory front including those of former US Federal Communications Commission Chairman Tom Wheeler. He argues that licensing advanced tech such as AI would be impractical and anti-competitive.[44] Yet, writes Wheeler, the licensing proposal does suggest some related answers: There must be technical and behavioural standards for the development and operation of AI tools, and there must be a dedicated regulator to develop and enforce those standards.[45]

The message is loud and clear; that the future of advanced and emerging technologies has to be built around both competition and safety. It's safe to agree with the proposition that we forget AI is a product of HI (human intelligence) at our peril.

Apart from being pervasive, rapid and non-linear, the technological transition is also, by definition, transient. This reinforces the need to build flexible and dynamic models to respond to changes and optimize benefits. Calibrating the application of advanced technologies without losing time while preparing for its adverse impacts is the central challenge India must overcome to tackle this transition successfully. This can be achieved by focusing on policies and practices that can help workers adapt to changing job requirements and ensure that the benefits of technology application are distributed broadly to prevent a further deepening of social cleavages.

Frontier technologies are at the cusp of becoming all-pervasive. Countries are focused, each according to its capacity, on enhancing their technological heft. The global contest therefore hinges on who can convert the adoption of frontier technologies into overall rise in productivity levels across the broad economic front, hastening the application of these technologies in day-to-day consumption, production and distribution functions.

It is increasingly evident that states of the so-called Third World which are unwilling or unable to bump up productivity using technology in key areas for knowledge-based innovation, are destined to remain in the low-tech category. But in the 'pluriverse of possibilities' the technology transition throws up on a near-daily basis, states that fully understand the implications of what's going on, are quick to define their national priorities, and ready to work hard to innovate, could yet prove surprise winners.[46]

India has all the components to emerge as a technology pioneer if all the three stakeholders can converge on the national priorities and operate on the same platform. Time, however, is of the essence—we are well past the 'wow' moment of the technological transition.

Globally, countries are beginning to reassess their strategic positions as the technological transition continues apace at a time of great uncertainty. So too must India. Influence over global trade, innovation and strategic capabilities will increasingly be premised on states' abilities to focus laser-like on the development and application of advanced technologies in priority areas.

A new form of geopolitical competition—where control over the digital ecosystem, data and algorithms become the key determinant of international influence, cooperation and alliances—is on the cards. Indeed, most technological disruptions leave both positive and negative effects in their wake. But only a handful of people seem to grasp the magnitude of the changes that are about to hit us, which, as a commentator iterated, 'are exciting—and terrifying.'

Let us put it like this: There's a reason why *Time* magazine, once known for coming up with a 'most influential people in the world' list each year with great fanfare, has now taken to publishing the *Time* 100 Most Influential People in AI list annually.[47]

Six

CLIMATE CONUNDRUM

Carbon Transition

It is absolutely true that India's young and still growing population needs cheap and affordable energy, better access to high-quality public transport, and adequate housing. It is, however, also absolutely true that if we continue to meet these legitimate demands by adopting a business-as-usual approach, our young population will suffer unimaginable damage to their health, livelihood and overall welfare as a result of increasing greenhouse gas (GHG) emissions and the consequent climate catastrophe.

This is the knife edge that India finds itself perched on precariously today. We daresay that, along with India, the entire Global South faces the same dilemma. We cannot afford to slow down our economic growth, especially for those at the bottom of the pyramid, nor can we not reduce our carbon footprint at the same time.

This chapter, perhaps audaciously, sets out to explore the imperative for our collective survival, to eliminate more carbon being released into the environment juxtaposed against the reality of economic inequalities, technology asymmetries, and geopolitical interests. If the world continues with business as usual, we have but a seven-year window after which we will go past the critical threshold set in COP15 Paris, of a 1.5°C rise in world temperatures above the average temperatures in the pre-Industrial Revolution period. Even for a more liberal target of limiting rise in global temperatures to below 2°C, the window is a mere twenty years. Therefore, only mitigation and adaptation strategies, while vital, just won't cut it anymore. The elimination of fresh carbon emissions and the removal of carbon already in the earth's atmosphere are now the critical imperatives for the health and wealth of nations.

The next section of this chapter briefly surveys the current state of the global environment challenge, which has been highlighted in COP 29 at Baku, Azerbaijan, the region where mineral oil was first sighted and used. We then examine the differentiated stance of advanced economies towards reducing carbon/GHG emissions—from complete denial *a la* Trump to an activist policy adopted by the European Union (EU), especially following the complete disruption of Russian fossil fuel supplies in the wake of the Ukraine conflict.

China has emerged as the world's largest GHG emitter—its annual emissions in 2023 were pegged at 13.97 billion tonnes as compared to second-placed US' 5.89 billion tonnes.[1] It is important, therefore, to discuss how China, which currently accounts for 32 per cent of total global emissions, is tackling the climate challenge. Beijing has initiated significant steps to reduce its emissions.[2] In the process, it has also created a near stranglehold on almost the entire supply chain for solar energy and electric vehicles (EVs), including access to critical minerals and rare earth elements that are essential for the global clean energy economy. Given the rise of China as a major player, we explore the key role of geopolitical, geoeconomic and technological factors in shaping the carbon transition.

In parsing the projected global energy mix over the next two decades, we have attempted to provide an evidence-based assessment of the relative importance of various energy sources. Against this backdrop, we raise the question of whether frontier technologies, for instance AI, contribute adversely to climate change or could their application reduce carbon emissions.

We then turn the focus on India, which faces a tricky carbon transition—both its economic growth and its citizens' welfare are at stake. About 25 per cent of our agriculture is at risk and our coastal regions are particularly vulnerable to the adverse impacts of global warming. Additionally, the Third Pole is melting, which could convert our perennial rivers to seasonal ones, with calamitous consequences especially in the densely populated Indo-Gangetic Plain.

In this context of enhanced climate vulnerability, we examine India's progress in the green economic transition and recommend policy priorities. What emerges repeatedly is that a business-as-usual mindset would damage India beyond repair. The need to evolve a new paradigm to tackle the carbon transition could not be more pressing. The next section proceeds to outline the possible strategic choices India will have to make as great power rivalry has thoroughly infiltrated the renewables-powered green energy domain; Delhi must work on a twin-track approach—domestic-facing and external.

Carbon reduction, elimination and removal will require a change in human behaviour. We have to thus question the 'hyper-consumerism culture' which is hard-wired in advanced economies head-on. Excessive consumption increases both emissions and the pace of ecological destruction. Our external engagement will have to adroitly avoid being caught in the midst of great power rivalry. Indeed, it would need to necessarily be premised on exercising our strategic autonomy to ensure that we can harness the technology and financing required for successfully tackling our simultaneous twin transition by adopting a source-agnostic approach. The final section of the chapter examines the options for India as it aspires to ensure OECD-comparable HDIs for its citizens at significantly lower levels of GDP. We postulate that Indians will need to dive deep into their traditions and behavioural norms and practices to achieve this difficult goal.

In conclusion, we suggest ways in which we can contribute to society evolving into a balanced co-existence with nature. We flag emerging ideas that are rapidly becoming mainstream across all societies, that could provide the basis for improving peoples' welfare while reducing our collective carbon footprint.

A Global Calamity in the Making

The emphasis of the IMF on the world needing to cut emissions by 25–50 per cent by 2030 compared to pre-2019 levels, to contain temperature rises to between 1.5 and 2 degrees Celsius, must be non-negotiable.[3] It is worth noting that even today rich countries are responsible for 82 per cent of total global emissions.[4]

Carbon reduction and temperature control must be universally seen as a global public good. Up to 18 per cent of the world's GDP could be wiped off by 2050 if global temperatures rise by 3.2°C, as will happen if present trends continue.[5] It will be apocalypse soon.

TABLE 1
The Impending Apocalypse

Temperature-rise scenario, by mid-century				
	Well-below 2°C increase	**2.0°C increase**	**2.6°C increase**	**3.2°C increase**
	Paris target	*The likely range of global temperature gains*		*Severe case*
Simulating for economic-loss impacts from rising temperatures in %GDP, relative to a world without climate change (0°C)				
World	–4.2%	–11.0%	–13.9%	–18.1%
OECD	–3.1%	–7.6%	–8.1%	–10.6%
North America	–3.1%	–6.9%	–7.4%	–9.5%
South America	–4.1%	–10.8%	–13.0%	–17.0%

Europe	−2.8%	-7.7%	-8.0%	−10.5%
Middle East & Africa	−4.7%	−14.0%	−21.5%	−27.6%
Asia	−5.5%	−14.9%	−20.4%	−26.5%
Advanced Asia	−3.3%	−9.5%	−11.7%	−15.4%
ASEAN	−4.2%	−17.0%	−29.0%	−37.4%
Oceania	−4.3%	−11.2%	−12.3%	−16.3%

Source: Swiss Re Institute: Climate Economics Index

But there is some visible respite from the impending apocalypse. A rising share of renewables in the primary energy mix by 2050 and a decline in the importance of fossil fuels have been forecast by BP in its Energy Outlook Report.[6] The share of renewable energy (RE) could grow to between 35 per cent and 60 per cent by 2050, from a mere 10 per cent in 2019. In the renewable energy mix, solar and wind power will expand rapidly and low-carbon hydrogen is also expected to play a critical role. Then there's nuclear energy. The share of fossil fuels is projected to slump to less than 50 per cent by 2050 from around 80 per cent in 2019.

Although the pace at which renewable energy will penetrate the global energy system is expected to be quicker than any previous fuel in history, the question surely is whether this is enough to stave off a major climatic disaster especially for the Global South.[7]

Nevertheless, such a scenario coming to fruition could upend current geopolitical alliances and energy security initiatives of major powers, and bring new actors into play. Recent geopolitical events such as the Russia-Ukraine war have showed how even relatively small disruptions to global energy supplies can lead to severe economic and social costs, making the strongest case for an 'orderly transition' away from hydrocarbons as nations pursue energy security by investing in renewables.[8]

The good news is the International Energy Agency's World

Energy Outlook (WEO) 2022 Report notes that we are at a historic turning point towards a cleaner energy system thanks to the unprecedented response across the world.[9] This includes the Inflation Reduction Act (IRA) of 2022 in the US, the Fit for 55 package and REPowerEU Plan in the European Union (EU), South Korea's efforts to increase the share of nuclear and renewables in its energy mix, and ambitious clean energy targets in China and India. Japan's Green Transformation (Gulf War) programme, too, has adopted stepped-up commitments that include a comprehensive vision of economic and energy security that views the current competition over green technology in the Indo-Pacific as crucial for future economic competitiveness.

The contrarian view holds that while rapid growth in renewable energy such as wind and solar will contribute to a more diversified global energy mix, fossil fuels like oil, natural gas and coal will continue to be the largest contributors, still providing 75 per cent of global energy demand in 2040.[10]

This view is clearly not a tenable global energy outlook. It will result in an unacceptable rise in global temperatures. This Trumpian view of the world is a nihilistic, self-fulfilling prophecy which leads to a doomsday scenario.

There is insufficient recognition that we are faced with an imminent closing of the climate change window. Experts tell us that this window is a maximum of twenty years long, after which we will likely reach the point of no return. Mere mitigation and adaptation efforts will clearly no longer suffice. This, even if there is agreement on the measures to be adopted and mobilization of sufficient financial resources to implement them. Eliminating carbon emissions and working on removing carbon already in the environment has therefore acquired criticality in the transition to a green future.

Unfortunately, as COP28 in Dubai showed, such an agreement

is nowhere in sight. In fact, the principal objective for COP 29, held in Baku, Azerbaijan, in November 2024, was to finalize plans for mobilizing necessary climate financing. That clearly did not happen.

The required volume of climate financing is estimated to be 10X of the amount ($100 billion per year) currently committed by COP participants. We are told that a miniscule $25 billion has so far been actually mobilized. No advanced economy has fulfilled its commitment thus far, and the Baku conference—held in the shadow of Trump's re-election as US President with a thumping majority—turned out to be a huge disappointment.[11] A paltry $300 billion per year was 'committed to in principle' by wealthy nations in Baku.[12]

Geopolitics and Energy Transition

The success or lack of it in the global energy system transformation (GEST) will be a key determinant of the transition away from carbon. A team of seven scholars led by Mathieu Blondeel of the Institute for Environmental Studies, Amsterdam, published an important paper in 2024—*Global Energy Scenarios: A Geopolitical Reality Check*—in which they explored the 'integration gap' that exists between Energy System Modelling and the stylized scenarios used therein, and energy geopolitics.[13]

Examining how these approaches may complement each other is essential for a further understanding of the future of the global energy system. The paper, using a qualitative analytical framework, reviews the extent to which a range of state-of-the-art global energy scenarios capture and reflect key issues in energy geopolitics in their narratives and model implementation.[14] Its findings: Few scenarios consider geopolitics in any depth. Those that do, often treat it as a barrier to the decarbonization efforts that are aligned with the climate objectives of the Paris Agreement.

'Normative, Paris-aligned scenarios describe smooth processes of change where cooperation and coordination between countries is assumed and where geopolitics is often completely absent,' write the authors. This assertion only serves to underline the need for a more intricate understanding of the difference between 'paper transitions' and the real-world messiness and complexities of GEST. In the real world, geopolitics has a 'dual quality' of simultaneously accelerating and hindering the transformation process.[15]

So, when advanced economies are in denial and unwilling to finance the costs of adaptation and mitigation, not to mention the removal of carbon already in the earth's atmosphere, it complicates matters further.

Achieving net-zero carbon emissions will require additional global investments of at least $1 trillion per year in energy infrastructure by 2030 and $3 trillion to $6 trillion across all sectors per year until 2050, by substantially reducing GHG emissions.[16] Additionally, according to one estimate, the annual climate adaptation costs in developing countries could reach $300 billion by 2030 and as much as $500 billion by 2050.[17] Emerging economies are also likely to be left with $290 billion to $580 billion in annual 'residual damages' by 2030 and over $1 trillion in such damages by 2050, from the impact of climate change that can't be prevented by adaptation measures.[18]

But the reality is that we have not yet even agreed on the distinction which must be made between the focus of the Global North on mitigating climate change by eliminating carbon emissions, and the need of developing countries for adaptation to the carbon already in the atmosphere. There is a long road ahead for any convergence of interests and views on the bouquet of measures required for achieving net-zero. It is vital for advanced economies to not just meet but exceed their annual pledge of providing climate finance for mitigation and adaptation measures predominantly to be taken in countries belonging to the Global South. Financing needed to meet adaptation and mitigation goals are estimated at trillions of dollars annually until 2050. But none of this happening.

Consensus on the volume of climate financing required and the measures to mobilize it, is as elusive as ever. It will surely become illusory as the Trump administration takes hold of US environment policy and reverses the advances made. We should, therefore, not expect any form of 'environment debt liquidation' from OECD countries which relentlessly pursue their Benthamite goal of maximizing consumption without thinking deeply about protecting the environment.

These affluent nations, without exception, have believed in and relied on the growth model of prioritizing material benefits *now* and retrofitting subsequently for ameliorating the resultant environmental damage. Horrific reminders of the consequences of such behaviour are strewn across the post-World War II global economic development landscape. The River Thames in London was so polluted during the 1950s and 1960s that it was a massive health risk to enter it unprotected. The Tokyo Bay disaster of the 1960s and 1970s, when the water was contaminated with mercury discharged from industrial units abutting its shore, required two decades of cleaning up. The worst living example is of the Aral Sea, the southern half of which simply dried up because the waters of the mighty Amu Darya (Oxus) could no longer drain into the sea. The toxic, chemical-laden soil from the dry seabed now swirls around large regions of Uzbekistan and Turkmenistan, causing extensive respiratory and other health problems. And yet, OECD member-states persist in their denial and pursue their short-sighted practice of 'saving themselves' from imported carbon. Hopefully, they will realize, sooner rather than later, that carbon emissions are a global public bad.

Some efforts have been undertaken by multilateral financial institutions to address the climate challenge. The Asian Development Bank (ADB), for instance, pledged $100 billion from its own resources over 2019–2030 to combat climate change in Asia.[19] The summit for the New Global Financing Pact in Paris, in June 2023, also agreed to find $200 billion in extra monies for low-income economies to be funnelled through the World Bank, which would have to take on more risk, a move that would require wealthy nations to inject more cash.[20] But even if and when this comes through—there is already debate around whether the World Bank retains the relevance to manage such an initiative—it might well end up as just a drop in the ocean.[21]

Calling for a 42 per cent cut in annual global GHG emissions by 2030 compared to 2019 levels to keep the world within 1.5 degrees Celsius of warming, the United Nations Environment Programme (UNEP) has underlined that the continuation of current policies will lead to a catastrophic temperature rise of 2.6–3.1 degrees Celsius over the course of this century above the pre-industrial (1850–1900) level.[22] In annual terms, the world needs to shave off 7.5 per cent of emissions every year until 2035. In sharp contrast to what is required, global emissions grew by 1.3 per cent year-on-year in 2023.[23] IMF analysis of current global climate targets shows we will deliver only an 11 per cent cut—less than half of the minimum reduction that is needed.[24]

In a business-as-usual scenario, middle- and low-income countries are expected to account for 66 per cent of global CO2 emissions by 2030, up from 44 per cent in 1990.[25] The effects of climate change are also expected to push an additional 130 million people into extreme poverty by 2030.[26] Global temperature rises will negatively impact GDP in all regions by the middle of the twenty-first century.

Central to the carbon transition is the rise of renewables and the future decline in the use of fossil fuels. Given that renewables differ in many respects from fossil fuels, it is safe to predict that these differences will have significant geopolitical consequences. According to the International Renewable Energy Agency (IRENA), renewable energy resources are available in one form or another in most countries, unlike fossil fuels which are concentrated in specific geographies. This reduces the importance of current energy choke points such as the narrow channels on widely used sea routes that are critical to the global supply of oil.[27]

Secondly, most renewables take the form of flows, while fossil fuels are stocks. Energy stocks can be stored, which is useful, but they can be used only once. In contrast, energy flows do not exhaust themselves and are harder to disrupt. Thirdly, renewable energy sources can be deployed at almost any scale and lend themselves better to decentralized forms of energy production and consumption. This adds to the democratizing effects of renewable energy. Fourthly, renewable energy sources have nearly zero marginal costs, and some of them, like solar and wind, enjoy cost reductions of nearly 20 per cent for every doubling of capacity.[28]

Last but not least, energy from renewable fuels being in the nature of flows has to be stored so that it can be utilized at a location and time that is different from the location and time of its generation. This calls for innovative solutions for storage technology, ones that can make renewables also a part of base load when the storage technology is further advanced, which in turn enhances their ability to drive change. But for this to come to fruition, regulatory solutions to ensure stability and profitability in the power sector are required.

The challenge, and it is a massive one, is the uneven pace of the energy transformation which is one of the major elements reshaping geopolitics in the twenty-first century. Reducing the global carbon footprint requires the developed world and major developing nations to work together (and take countries most vulnerable to climate change along). That is, realistically, possible only if mutually profitable outcomes are both assured and quantifiable.

Given these realities and the real-world messiness and self-serving attitude of advanced economies and their persistent denial of the environment debt they owe to the Global South, it is becoming increasingly evident that developing countries may have to come together for mobilizing the necessary financial and technological resources to accelerate carbon elimination and removal from the environment. After all, it is the developing world which faces an existential issue vis-à-vis the looming climate catastrophe.

A Clash of Transitions

But how is the Global South expected to address the new environmental threats that are emerging with the rise of AI, which is being ruthlessly promoted by Big Tech in OECD countries?

These are threats being foisted on the world without a thought to their impact on further shortening the climate window. For example, an argument now gaining traction is that Big Tech cannot and/or will not contribute to ameliorating the disastrous impact of climate change and ever-growing social inequality.

An increasing number of experts are also taking the position that AI's potential climate cost as energy demand surges amid the data-centre race is not fully understood. AI's appetite for electricity and water is becoming insatiable as models get larger.[29] *Nikkei Asia* writes 'everyone acknowledges that AI is having an increased (negative) impact on the environment.'[30]

TABLE 2

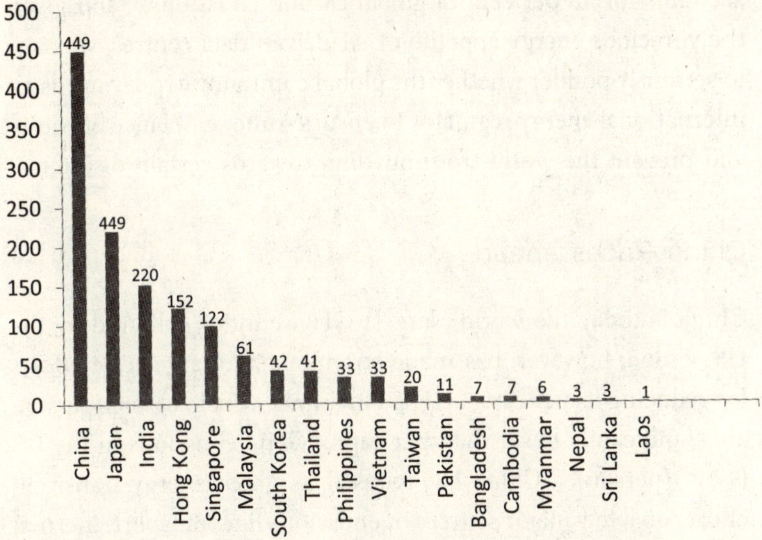

As the above chart shows, burgeoning data centres in Asia are the main cause for AI energy consumption. These so-called 'central brains' are used to power countries' digital needs and much of the environmental impact is in the accelerated construction of new data centres, as well as the ongoing demand for energy and water.[31]

Between 2022 and 2026, the total electricity consumption of global data centres is forecast to double, reaching more than 1,000 terawatt hours in 2026. That's equivalent to the entire current annual energy consumption of Japan.[32]

Yet, the environmental cost of AI when economic leadership is at stake is being ignored as many policymakers believe—and the authors agree—that AI resources will be decisive factors that drive countries' overall economic and geopolitical competitiveness.[33] A Clash of Transitions—technology versus climate change—is thus on the anvil.

When the richest 10 per cent of the world's population accounts for 48 per cent of global carbon emissions,[34] and given the voracious energy appetite of AI-driven data centres, we have to seriously ponder whether the global community today needs an international energy regulator to ensure some semblance of equity and prevent the world from hurtling towards certain disaster.

China Races ahead

China is today the world's largest GHG emitter, followed by the US. China, however, has made strenuous and large-scale efforts for reducing its per capita GHG emissions, which, at 9.8 t/person, are significantly lower than per capita GHG emissions in the US (17.2 t/person).[35] China has focused its green energy transition efforts on a few major sources of emissions like transport, thermal power generation from burning coal, and massive deployment of both large-scale solar energy farms and decentralized rooftop solar energy generation.

China's progress in clean, coal-based thermal power generation is widely recognized for its success in enabling the country to harness its vast coal reserves for electricity generation.[36] It has taken an enormous lead over other countries in converting both the private and public transport from being a largely fossil-fuel-based system to one driven predominantly by electricity. Its 27,000 km long high-speed passenger rail network, developed over the last 25 years, now connects all provincial capitals and ensures that the growth in air traffic, which is high on GHG emissions, is reduced. The 100 per cent electrification of railway tracks has resulted in a rising share of freight being moved by rail compared to roads.

The growth in the production of EVs in China has been simply astounding. Chinese EV companies including biggies like

BYD and Geely have captured over 60 per cent of the global market for EVs.[37] Around six million electric two-wheelers (e2W) were sold in China in 2023, and the country accounted for 78 per cent of global sales of e2Ws in that year.[38] (All this, despite the pandemic-related disruption of supply chains and consequent slowdown.) Chinese cities periodically announce bans on petrol-driven two-wheelers (2Ws), especially in city centres, and have mandates to promote EV use.

As a result of these efforts and more, China is likely reducing the growth of its GHG emissions, which could be entering an extended period of structural decline due to record growth in the installation of new low-carbon energy sources.[39] Among major economies, India in FY23 recorded the steepest increase in GHG emissions climbing 6.1 per cent, according to the UNEP *Emissions Gap Report 2024*.[40]

It is estimated that China requires $26 trillion green investment by 2050 to reach its goal of carbon neutrality, ahead of national climate targets. According to UNEP, it is on track to succeed in meeting its 2030 goals. China has spent 20 years building a rare earth elements/critical minerals supply chain especially focused on Africa and is looking for deposits in ever newer geographies, including Afghanistan, Kazakhstan, Mongolia and parts of Latin America. Rare earth elements and critical minerals are essential components for a host of renewable energy technologies that have cross-sectoral applications and are critical to the global green energy transition.

China leads the world in the acquisition of these assets. It commands a massive lead in renewable energy manufacturing capacity, more than what even OPEC does in oil, which controls close to 40 per cent of global oil production.[41] China produces over 50 per cent of the world's lithium and nickel, as well as 70 per cent of cobalt, extending China's lead upstream. It refines 60 per cent of the world's lithium and is responsible for 60 per cent of global production of rare earths as well as 85 per cent of their processing capacity—the global demand for rare earths is forecast to reach 315,000 tonnes by 2030.[42] And Beijing has supply well in hand; China is today the world's largest supplier of clean technology products.[43]

Bridging the Finance Gap

Slowing and reversing climate change and emissions require trillions of dollars of financing. China, a pivotal player in the global economy, is already moving to fund the climate transition through innovative financing mechanisms, writes climate change scholar Sha Song.[44] These innovative financial mechanisms include MYbank, a technology-driven internet bank incubated by Alibaba, which created a special financing platform for 6.23 million micro and small-sized enterprises. As of 2023, MYbank offered preferential interests on loans for 420,000 micro and small enterprises, advancing their green development while providing them with easy-to-access inclusive financial services. It has also developed a range of new green finance products based on customer needs and formed a green and digital supply chain finance-product matrix, including green procurement loans.[45]

Bridging the finance gap needs precisely the kind of innovation Beijing is implementing for decarbonization of the domestic industrial value chain. A case in point is low-carbon technology (upstream and downstream), which is a significant enabler along the value chain that at different stages requires customized or tailor-made financial tools.[46] In fact, China is successfully positioning itself as best-placed to help deliver and scale up low-carbon technologies and foster innovation chains to emerging/developing economies.

Beijing is leveraging the fact that it is the main trading partner of about 140 countries and is thus well positioned to define the pace of the green transition of the global supply chain.[47] According to the International Energy Agency (IEA), between 2017 and 2022 the demand from the energy sector was the factor behind a tripling in overall demand for lithium, a 70 per cent jump in demand for cobalt, and a 40 per cent rise in demand for nickel.[48] In 2022, the share of clean energy applications in total demand reached 56 per cent for lithium, 40 per cent for cobalt, and 16 per cent for nickel (up from 30 per cent for lithium, 16 per cent for cobalt, and 6 per cent for nickel, from five years ago).[49]

This dominance puts China in pole position in the transition away from carbon. The world's dependency on China for renewables has, predictably, sparked a backlash led by the US, which sees its dependence on China for supply of renewable energy components as a national security threat. It is, therefore, pursuing a policy in tandem with its allies for coming up with alternate RE sources and technological solutions that are not dependent on critical minerals.[50]

Such a policy, even as Trump shows signs of doubling down on it with or without the support of US allies, will backfire, say academics David G. Victor and Michael R. Davidson. They insist that tariffs and barriers that restrict Chinese companies from doing business in the US prevent American companies from accessing the world's top innovations and limit their ability to help redefine the technological frontier with their own ideas.[51] This warning holds true for India as well.

But there appears to be limited traction for this view in Washington or Delhi policy circles despite experts iterating that a tariff war between the world's two biggest economies over clean energy technologies is a zero-sum game when it comes to the carbon transition. The rest of the world—including India if it continues to ignore the necessity of working with China, even if with teeth gritted—will not be immune to such a fait accompli. At the same time, it will be critical for countries to cooperate on developing alternate RE sources like green hydrogen, nuclear fusion and plasma, and environmentally safe hydropower, and promoting the deployment of small modular reactors (SMRs).

The Great Game of Climate

The US-led pushback to China's dominance is taking multiple forms. Washington is making a concerted effort to woo African countries that have rich reserves of critical minerals/rare earth.[52] But Beijing has already made substantial inroads in the continent.[53] Further, while the US is trying to woo mineral-rich African nations, its own domestic legislation in the form of the Inflation Reduction Act has arguably had the effect of shutting out African countries from becoming a part of the US green energy transition.[54]

There's also an attempt being made to promote the Asia-Pacific Economic Cooperation (APEC) as a forum for shared standards in critical mineral exploitation and trade. But US-China rivalry is playing out in APEC too, making progress difficult.

The efforts initiated within the Quad by US-Australia, on the other hand, are focused around the logic that with a number of nations aiming for net-zero emissions targets between 2050 and 2070, a massive supply of critical minerals will be the prerequisite to build the commodities and infrastructure architecture required for supporting a lower-carbon energy network. Each interlocking facet of energy production, trade and consumption thus relies on the stability of existing partnerships and processes.[55]

The US-led Minerals Security Partnership (MSP), a sans-China attempt at global rulemaking by the developed world to ensure critical minerals are produced, processed and recycled to secure supply chains and weaken China's grip on supplies of critical minerals, is the counter to Beijing's dominance. India is the only developing country to have been invited to join the multinational pact.

To sum up, given China's considerable advances in its green energy transition, it will be useful, perhaps imperative, for India to explore options of technology transfer both in clean coal power generation and EVs. While we must of course strongly persist with our own indigenous efforts for evolving alternate green energy generation technologies, it will do us no harm to shorten our transition cycle by acquiring such technologies from China. Therefore, in the realm of the energy transition, as perhaps in the geostrategic domain, India will do well to maintain its strategic autonomy. We must adopt the optimal solutions for our successful carbon transition, irrespective of their provenance.

India: Tricky Transition

India's nominal per capita income has risen nearly 7X from $369 in 1990 to $2,485 (current US$) in 2023.[56] In PPP terms, the rise looks even more impressive.[57] Despite this significant growth, India ranks 124th among 200 countries in per capita income terms.[58]

At these income levels and given the fairly skewed income distribution, the lower deciles of its population are certainly incapable of achieving the desired levels of HDIs. Therefore, it is imperative that India at the bare minimum quadruples the per capita income levels of its lowest deciles for them to afford at least an acceptable standard of living. At the same time, India's total GHG emissions, presently at 3 gigatonnes (GTs) of carbon dioxide equivalent (CO2eq), are doubling every eight years. At this rate, they will reach an unsustainable 12 GTs by 2040 and an incredible 24 GTs by 2048. This will surely not allow us to achieve our net-zero target by 2070; we have to slow down the growth of GHG emissions beginning now.

It is estimated that climate change can deplete India's GDP by 2.6 per cent by 2100 even while capping the global temperature rise below 2°C—in a scenario of global temperature increases to 4°C, this depletion is estimated at 13.4 per cent.[59] Economies in South and Southeast Asia are among the most susceptible to the physical risks associated with global warming. Countries most negatively impacted—including India—are often the ones with the least resources to mitigate and adapt to the effects of global warming. On the flip side, these countries also have the most to gain from global efforts to reduce temperature rises. Climate-related natural disasters between 2000 and 2019, a significant proportion of them in the Global South, claimed 1.23 million lives and levied an economic cost of $2.97 trillion, an exponential rise from previous decades.[60] (2023 was also the warmest year on record at 1.45 ± 0.12 °C above the pre-industrial average.)

In India, where agriculture is still a large sector, the demand for more irrigation to feed a large population with changing food habits is leading to a rapidly receding water table. India is the largest user of groundwater globally, extracting more than the US and China put together.[61] In 2022, as many as 63 per cent of India's districts reported falling groundwater levels. In many cases, the aquifers are getting contaminated with arsenic and heavy metals. Poverty rates are up to 10 per cent higher in districts where groundwater tables have fallen below eight metres, leaving small farmers particularly vulnerable.[62] If current trends persist, the World Bank estimates at least 25 per cent of India's agriculture will be at risk.

While agriculture everywhere is affected by changing climatic parameters (temperature, rainfall, humidity, etc.), farming in coastal regions is additionally vulnerable to seawater intrusion, cyclones, and an increase in soil salinity. The change in climatic parameters has adversely affected the phenology of plants in almost all the coastal parts of India—erratic rainfall coupled with an increased temperature regime has already disrupted the traditional cropping pattern.[63]

In fact, India's vast coastline of over 7,500 km is among the geographies most susceptible to the alarming impact of climate change/variability and sea-level rise due to global warming. The high density of population in India's coastal areas and their low adaptive capacity make the unfolding impact of climate-induced changes very ominous indeed.

Smallholder farming communities in coastal areas need urgent help in both adapting to climate change and adopting climate-smart strategies. The fisheries sector is feeling the impact already. It is estimated that the ecosystem services of the East Coast are expected to decrease by 25 per cent by 2050, resulting in an overall loss of at least $17 billion.[64] This only serves to highlight the need for effective mitigation strategies.

The consequences of continued carbon emissions won't fall solely on rural and coastal communities. According to climate modelling projections by NASA, sea-level rise by 2030 will inundate the 10 major coastal cities of India, including Mumbai and Chennai. Climate change-induced sea-level rise will also pose a serious threat to the 12 major and 200-odd minor/intermediate Indian ports, impacting trade.[65] Likely mass migration by internally displaced peoples, including those from Bangladesh, will put severe pressure on already inadequate infrastructure, and the prospect of violent societal upheaval in India could become acute.

For the billion-plus human population of the northern part of the Indian subcontinent and southern China, on the other hand, the Himalayan, Karakoram and Hindu Kush high mountain ranges are the most reliable water source. Glaciers and snow in these mountains contain the largest volume of fresh water outside of Earth's polar ice sheets, leading hydrologists to term this region the Third Pole. According to NASA, one-seventh of the world's population depends on the water of rivers flowing from these mountains.[66]

But rapid changes in the region's climate are affecting glacier and snow melt; residents are already modifying their land-use practices in response to the changing water supply. The 'Asian Brown Cloud'—the name given to a form of atmospheric haze that is the result of toxic airborne chemicals including black carbon, soot and fly-ash resulting from the burning of fossil fuels/crop residue—covers the Himalayas both in India and China every winter. This results in large and rising carbon deposits on the snow-covered peaks, which absorb more sunlight, raising temperatures and accelerating the snow melt. Its impact can be seen in the more rapid shrinkage of glaciers, with the imminent risk of the perennial water flow of major rivers being interrupted.

This could be devastating for the large populations of the region which are dependent on river-borne irrigation. The region's ecology is transforming, which has significant consequences for food and water security in India, China and other Asian nations.

The core issue which thus needs highlighting in the carbon transition is that neither mitigation measures taken by developed economies nor adaptation by emerging economies will suffice to meet the desired goals. Both developed and emerging economies will now have to work together to prevent further carbon emissions and the removal of carbon that is already in the environment.

Between Policy and Pretence

The enormity of India's twin challenge of rapid income growth and slowing down the increase of its GHG emissions should be evident from the above brief description. For Delhi to accomplish this dual objective will require out-of-the-box policy thinking, domestically grown product and process innovations, and the mobilization of substantial financial resources and skills. India will also have to negotiate the clash of transitions as it attempts to use frontline technology including AI while at the same time reduce its carbon footprint and navigate the ongoing global geostrategic transition. It is a steep hill to climb. But it has to be done. Only a whole-of-society approach, implemented urgently and with imagination, that brings all relevant stakeholders together pulling in the same direction, can produce the desired results.

While many emerging markets (EMs), including India, have put in place ambitious intended nationally determined contributions (INDCs), the realization of these climate goals will be constrained by development imperatives which are linked to the availability and quality of capital within their reach. According to an estimate, India will need $2.5 trillion till 2030 to meet its INDC goals.[67]

Delhi has reiterated that it is committed to achieving the net-zero emissions target by 2070 as announced by PM Modi as part of the *Panchamrit Declaration* at COP26. India says it is on track to deliver on its INDCs, including turning net-zero by 2070 and reducing emission intensity by 33–35 per cent by 2030 against 2005 levels. 'We have achieved our commitment of 40% energy production from renewable sources, way ahead of the 2030 Paris Agreement target,' a Cabinet minister asserted in late 2023.[68] (At the COP26 summit in Glasgow, India had updated its INDCs under the Paris Agreement of 2015 and its long-term low-carbon development strategies towards net-zero emissions by 2070.)

However, India witnessed a significant spike in GHG emissions (6.1 per cent y-o-y) in 2023,[69] and its carbon emissions are set to peak only in 2045–47, despite a strategy built on enhancing the installed capacity of renewable energy and the electrification of end-use sectors. India is third after China and the US in GHG emissions, the UNEP's Emissions Gap Report 2024 underlined.[70]

So, where does all this leave us? First, we have to find a way to work with China as well as the US and its allies. India's success or failure in this respect will be the true test of its strategic autonomy. Secondly, India must speed up the development of its own capacity for exploration for and excavation of critical minerals and rare earths within the country and abroad.

India's choices in transitioning away from carbon will directly influence its ability to improve citizens' wealth and health, carrying intergenerational—and potentially irreversible—consequences. We must hasten transitioning to a green economy, and do so prioritizing the limited funds available to mitigate the impact of carbon already in the environment, while simultaneously designing policies and programmes aimed at helping citizens adapt to climate change. As for our engagement with the rest of the world, it would necessarily be predicated on underlining carbon emissions elimination as a global issue for which international cooperation is essential, on which could be premised a new era of globalization.

Creating awareness on the need to recognize the criticality of carbon elimination as being both in the national interest as well as a crucial global public good, therefore, suggests itself as the central plank for Indian policymaking. Managing this most vital of transitions, while focusing on our development imperatives, is the key to success. Bridging the chasm between the stands of the BASIC (Brazil, South Africa, India, China) bloc and leading OECD nations on carbon footprints is an exemplar of the challenges going forward.

Gathering the Fireflies

The need for India to evolve a new paradigm to tackle the carbon transition cannot be put off any longer. There are many innovative initiatives being undertaken in both the public and private sector. Now is the time to bring them all together and scale them up massively, thereby gathering the fireflies.

Green Transition in Energy Supply

Officially published figures peg India's installed RE capacity as of 2022 at 150.54 GW (solar: 48.55 GW, wind: 40.03 GW, small hydro: 4.83 GW, biopower: 10.62 GW, large hydro: 46.51 GW). India's nuclear energy-based installed capacity stood at 6.78 GW. This brings the total non-fossil-based installed energy capacity to 157.32 GW, which is 40.1 per cent of the total installed electricity capacity of 392.01 GW at the time.

India upgraded its commitments under its INDCs at Glasgow COP26, and in August 2022 communicated its updated INDCs to the UNFCCC.[71] These include:

(i) Reducing emissions intensity of GDP by 45 per cent by 2030 (from 2005 levels)

(ii) Attaining 50 per cent cumulative electric power installed capacity from non-fossil-fuel-based energy resources by 2030, with the help of transfer of technology and low-cost international finance including from Green Climate Fund (GCF)

The power sector shows immense promise with the advent of green hydrogen as a viable clean energy source. Hydrogen is considered the second-most important form of energy carrier next to electricity. And green hydrogen could be a critical enabler of the global transition to sustainable energy and net-zero emission economies. There is unprecedented momentum around the world to fulfil hydrogen's longstanding potential as a clean energy solution.

It needs underlining that the role of policy and technology innovation is vital for building clean energy industries, as evidenced in the successes of renewable energy technologies and EVs. While a roadmap was put in place by India with the publication of the National Green Hydrogen Mission document in January 2023, it is now time to switch from mission-mode to action-mode for India to achieve a clean, secure and affordable energy future.

The achievement of the mission's objectives, the Indian government acknowledges, requires a comprehensive strategy that coordinates efforts across multiple sectors. Therefore, the mission strategy comprises interventions for:

(i) demand creation by making green hydrogen produced in India competitive for exports and for domestic consumption;
(ii) addressing supply-side constraints through an incentive framework; and
(iii) building an enabling ecosystem to support scaling and development.[72]

Hydrogen is also emerging as one of the leading options for storing energy from renewables, with hydrogen-based fuels offering the potential to transport that energy over long distances. Green hydrogen can be a means to decarbonize heavy industry, long-haul freight, shipping and aviation.

Hydropower is another focus area for India, with hydroelectric power projects totalling 15 GW of capacity currently under construction. The government expects hydro capacity to increase from 42 GW today to 67 GW by 2031–32, marking an increase of more than 50 per cent.[73]

Given the ongoing energy transitions in the country, the

development of pumped storage projects (PSPs) is vital for providing greater inertia and balancing power to the grid. Also known as water batteries, PSPs complement clean energy systems. PSPs with an aggregate capacity of 2.7 GW are under construction currently in India, and another 50 GW capacity is in various stages of development. As per government projections, PSP capacity will increase from 4.7 GW to around 55 GW by 2031–32.[74]

Nonetheless, the unpredictability of hydro as an energy source cannot be denied. There was a sharp fall in hydropower generation in 2023–24 when compared to 2022–23. (The causes range from less than normal rainfall in South India to natural disasters in other parts.)[75] The share of hydropower in India's total installed capacity stands at 10.4 per cent currently,[76] and by 2031–32 it is projected to come down to 7.51 per cent.[77] Yet, the importance of hydro to a power system which has begun the energy transition cannot be underestimated. Taken together with the potentially critical contribution of solar power—India surged to third in the world in terms of solar power generation in 2023[78]—and wind power to the current energy mix, hydropower must continue to provide essential support to the electricity grid, enhancing its reliability and resilience.

The share of solar power in India's total installed capacity is 19.8 per cent and that of wind power 10.5 per cent as of today.[79] The former is projected to register a massive jump to 40.49 per cent by 2031–32, while over the same period the latter is expected to inch up to 13.54 per cent.[80] Vitally, the share of coal in India's total installed capacity (46.80 per cent currently)[81] is forecast to drop sharply to 28.84 per cent by 2031–32.[82]

The encouragement in Budget 2024 for rooftop solar energy with the provision of 300 units of free energy will also help the country minimize its carbon footprint as it increases its energy production by 2–3X in the coming decades. Such a large increase is required to bring the Indian consumer at par with the global average energy consumption which stood at 21,394 kWh in 2023. Energy use per person for 2023 in India was 7,586 kWh, in the US it was 77,028 kWh, and in China 33,267 kWh. A massive expansion in installed energy-generating capacity and in generation levels is clearly a necessary development imperative in India for improving the quality of life for its people. Developing technologies to produce 'clean coal' is also worth pursuing.

Small modular reactors too need to be commissioned expeditiously regardless of fringe protests. The budgetary allocation for R&D for such reactors is a positive step as they may be the best substitute for the base load currently provided by coal-based power plants. Transfer of technology by global private companies, which may have already made substantial advances in small modular nuclear reactor (SMNRs), needs to be prioritized.

Green Transition in Energy Demand

In its revised submission to UNFCCC in August 2022, India has committed to propagating a healthy and sustainable way of living based on traditions and values of conservation and moderation, including through the LiFE (Lifestyle for Environment) movement, to help combat climate change.

As India rapidly urbanizes, carbon-positive construction and new green building materials will be needed. Moreover, a clear strategy is required for the de-carbonization of hard-to-abate sectors including steel and cement. Speeding up the move to de-carbonize transport must also be high on the list of priorities for India, as should be a continuous and continuing emphasis on the 'Refuse (lower consumption targets), Reuse, Recycle' campaign.

This will help change patterns of private consumption. Campaigns focused on energy saving, like the eleven-year-long yatra being undertaken by Professor Chetan Solanki of IIT Bombay,[83] have to be widely replicated and greatly scaled. We have to effectively and urgently translate the 'nationally determined targets' to 'privately determined targets'. In a devoutly-to-be-wished-for scenario, government action should be supplemented with strong individual commitment for achieving our national goals.

Last but by no means least, is the pressing issue of the agriculture sector and whether our current model is sustainable. In this respect, regenerative or natural farming and its role in carbon sequestration and in improving farmers' health and income levels has perhaps not received the attention it deserves. The hypothesis that natural farming is a potent tool for carbon removal from the environment, while also adequately addressing India's food security requirements, needs urgent and rigorous testing.

Dharma over Development

The onus is now on Delhi to robustly articulate a twin-track approach. First, it should aim to expedite domestic-oriented efforts in carbon elimination/removal by implementing measures mentioned discussed above, stepping up public awareness, and also bolstering the demand side of RE which has massive employment-generation potential. Secondly, India must initiate a global campaign to take leadership of the carbon elimination mission and emerge as a climate warrior nation with its resultant enhanced soft power contributing to augmenting the country's international standing.

In an ideal world, the carbon transition would have been managed optimally if we all followed Ladakh's (or Bhutan's, for that matter) model and 'put dharma over development'.[84] Unfortunately, we live in a fractious world where access to each resource is bitterly contested and competition for immediate financial benefit rules.

We are not naïve enough to believe that the goodness of human beings will spontaneously combust and we will all live happily ever after. But neither can we be blasé about the terror and devastation that awaits us if the transition away from carbon is not prioritized. *The Uninhabitable Earth: Life After Warming* by David Wallace-Wells makes the case in supremely lyrical prose, as a reviewer underlined, for our pending Armageddon.[85]

We fear that the world is reaching a stage where unless rich countries do more than just issue an apologia for their rapacious post-Industrial Revolution development models on which their current prosperity in large measure rests, the Global South may slip into adopting a nihilistic approach towards the carbon transition. The consequences of rich nations refusing to pay up, and developing nations adopting a damn-us-all-then-because-we-have-to-grow-rapidly approach, means disaster for all humanity.

Traditional Indian practices, cutting across class, caste, religion and region, have emphasised that exclusively hankering after and/or single-mindedly pursuing material demands, which are more often than not simply insatiable, cannot give us the happiness that we aspire for. Instead, it has been the longstanding Indian ethos to achieve equanimity, and perchance bliss, while preserving nature and the environment.

Such behavioural patterns, though, are under significant pressure as India's middle-class expands and sees its success in aping the conspicuous, wasteful and ostentatious consumerism of advanced economies. This is truly ironic as the strongly emerging behavioural trend in these economies is to cut back on material consumption and (re)connect with nature.

The need for India to fashion policies that help it address the huge challenge of simultaneously growing its economy so as to meet citizens' rational material aspirations while reducing its carbon footprint, lies at the very heart of a successful transition.

That such a policy architecture be flexible and tailored to the diverse requirements of India's variegated regions and states will be an additional policy-design requirement.

EPILOGUE

Turning Crisis into Catalyst

It is worth reiterating that never before in the history of global economic development did countries have to contend with such enormous challenges while pursuing their development agenda. This implies that there is no standard model or blueprint that India or other countries in the Global South can emulate to complete their own economic transition. Ignoring these challenges and pursuing a development paradigm that simply imitates the linear path followed by the present set of advanced economies could result in nasty surprises and unbearable human costs.

Following the business-as-usual model could indeed result in a catastrophic infringement of planetary boundaries. India's leadership has to mobilize all necessary talents and resources to design and implement a development strategy that innovatively responds to these multiple challenges and effectively exploits the opportunities that are inherent in the evolving trends for meeting our national goals.

The Rediscovery of India

In order to chart a feasible development path while engaging with the extant challenges, it is imperative to clearly define the national goal that the policy seeks to achieve. The long-term development goal for India must be to meet the exploding aspirations of its young population. This is broadly captured in the term *Viksit Bharat* propagated by Prime Minister Modi. But as is increasingly evident, there can be several interpretations of *Viksit Bharat*. And hence, it is important to define as clearly as possible the actual contours of India as a developed economy.

The highest level of aspiration for Viksit Bharat would be to restore India's position in the world economy by 2050—which would mark the centenary of India emerging as a sovereign republic—as it was prior to being colonized in 1850. This would imply increasing its share in the world economy from the present 3 per cent to 18 per cent, which according to Angus Maddison was India's share in 1850, over the next 25 years.[1] With the global GDP estimated to easily cross $200 trillion by 2050, India's GDP will have to be over $36 trillion from the present $3.8 trillion, requiring an annual average growth rate of about 9 per cent over the next two-and-a-half decades.[2] We have to face the reality that this level of ambition to reverse the historical injustice and colonial exploitation may take longer.

Perhaps it is more relevant to aim for India to raise its share in the global economy back to pre-colonial times in terms of PPP as that yields a more accurate estimate of people's welfare status. In PPP terms, the global economy in 2050 is estimated to expand to $268 trillion. To achieve a share of 18 per cent in this PPP-based global economy, the Indian economy will have to grow to $48 trillion in PPP terms by 2050.

According to the World Bank, the current (2023) size of the Indian economy in PPP terms is $14.6 trillion. The Indian economy will thus have to achieve and average an annual rate of growth (in PPP terms) of 5 per cent to regain its share of 18 per cent in the global economy. This, of course, is eminently possible and doable. In all likelihood, the Indian performance will be better over the next two-and-a-half decades.

However, we cannot take this as our development goal because a country's CNP and actual standing in the global community is based on the size and composition of its nominal economy. Therefore, given India's strengths, talents and innovative capabilities, this ambition of reclaiming its share in the global economy in nominal terms must be kept in place. Positing this goal could serve to forge the much-needed whole-of-society consensus and coherence on the shape and intensity of the national effort required for India to successfully tackle the six global transitions occurring simultaneously and reach developed-economy status by 2050.

Another, perhaps more achievable, interpretation of *Viksit Bharat* could be to try and complete by 2050 India's transition from a low-middle-income country, which we are at present, to join the ranks of the high-income countries as defined by the World Bank. This will require per capita incomes to rise from the present \$2,880 to \$14,001 by 2050.[3] The average annual rate of growth required to achieve this transition to a high-income economy will be 6.5 per cent. India has already attained an average annual growth of 7.8 per cent between 1990–91 (GDP \$321 billion) and 2023–24 (GDP \$3,900 billion). So, achieving an average annual growth rate of 6.5 per cent may appear to be an easy target. But conditions today are different from the decade of the 1990s and the first two decades of the present century.

The world economy is far more fragmented and is not growing as rapidly as it did during the previous three decades. Owing to protectionist concerns and the COVID-induced focus on 'near/onshoring', growth of global trade has markedly slowed down and is no longer assured to be higher than global GDP growth. China has already emerged as the major manufacturing power with 35 per cent share in gross global manufacturing,[4] leaving a very restricted space for India to grow its manufacturing exports and use exports as a driver of labour-intensive economic growth. The AI revolution, while opening some growth opportunities, could also imply large-scale loss of jobs both domestically and for Indians seeking to work in advanced economies. And most importantly, India will have to achieve this required sustained growth rate of nearly seven per cent while reducing its carbon footprint and restraining its per capita emissions of GHGs.

A third version of India's vision for 2050 could be to ensure that the entire population reaches human development indicators that are comparable to those achieved by OECD economies without necessarily achieving OECD levels of per capita incomes. This will perhaps be required because India cannot possibly reach OECD levels of per capita incomes without making a catastrophic impact on the planetary environment conditions. Therefore, a far more focused approach on improving the living conditions of its large population, especially those at the bottom of the pyramid, will have to be pursued in the coming period. This is also the objective of the Lifestyle for Environment (LiFE) launched by Prime Minister Modi at Glasgow COP26 when he committed India to attain net-zero status by 2070. The goal of providing globally comparable human development indicators for its entire population that will peak at 1.7 billion while realizing per capita incomes that are markedly lower than OECD economies, will require a bold and innovative way of designing the development blueprint for the country.

Therefore, India will have to find its own model of development that combines high economic growth with lower emissions and a focus on providing equitable living conditions for its population, especially those at the bottom of the pyramid. Adherence to this principle makes it imperative that those in the last income decile have similar HDIs as the rest of the population, which will result in an immediate reduction of the extent of inequity in society. Contrary to the earlier (now pretty much rejected) understanding that rapid growth necessarily comes at the cost of higher inequity, recent work by Thomas Piketty, Dani Rodrik, et.al., has shown that improving equity is a necessary condition for improving overall welfare levels in any society. In fact, it may be argued, Pandit Deendayal Upadhyay's postulate of *Antyodaya* should be seen as a precursor to the current focus on improving equity levels for achieving desirable development outcomes.

To be able to do so, India may well have to move away from a single-minded pursuit of GDP growth, which completely ignores equity considerations and could, in fact, result in policies that consciously worsen equity while hoping to achieve higher material growth. An example would be a continuous reduction in tax on corporate profits for encouraging private investors while cutting public expenditure on basic health and primary education that would benefit the poorer segments of society.

Our own ethos and ethics militate against such a concept of economic progress that focuses only on material growth irrespective of the source of this growth, which could include criminal activities like manufacturing illicit drugs, or the damage that such material growth may inflict on society and nature. We have traditionally been worshippers of nature and our creed has been for humans to live in consonance with nature and not to either conquer or destroy it for our material advantage. As Dattopant Thengadi, a leading voice arguing for the adoption of an Indian philosophy of development, says, we have to also consider the vital inputs by Indian women (albeit in traditional societal-familial structures) in maintaining family welfare, skilling the younger generation, and preserving societal stability. Such is the Indian ground reality. GDP growth as currently estimated does not include the contribution of very large segments of the female population in its calculations.

For all these reasons, which can be amplified further, it is time to replace Simon Kuznets' age-old but now outdated concept[5]—because of the changes in our understanding of what constitutes human welfare—with an alternative formulation that better reflects a society's true level of welfare.

It is thus important that India joins countries like France and Bhutan in reimagining and redefining the aggregate measure of peoples' welfare.[6] A way forward would be to construct the index of gross welfare product (GWP) as a measure of the real level of people's welfare with the following components:

(i) growth in per capita incomes;
(ii) progress towards achieving net-zero or the annual reduction in per capita emissions;
(iii) educational attainments as measured by enrolment ratios from primary to higher education and a measure of the quality of learning at various stages;
(iv) composite health indicators that reflect overall health status but focus more sharply on children's and mothers' health conditions;
(v) access to public services, including DPI; and
(vi) the rate of growth in per capita income of the last decile of the population.

India should try and create a 'Coalition of the Willing' within the G20 framework to complete the necessary conceptual work in creating the GWP index and also undertake the initial estimation in G20 countries.

We would prefer the adoption of GWP and achieving OECD-comparable indicators in the human development index as the definition for *Viksit Bharat* to be attained by 2050.

We now have an understanding of the six global challenges

that India has to face and navigate while it pursues its long-term national goal of ensuring that the lowest decile of its population attains OECD-comparable levels of HDIs over the next 25 years. This provides us the conceptual framework for discussing the necessary steps for India to achieve its goal of becoming *viksit*, or developed, when it celebrates the centenary of becoming a sovereign republic.

NITI Ashtanga: The Eight-Fold Path

Having a clear idea of the enormity of the challenges confronting us simultaneously, we suggest an eight-fold path of fundamental reforms that will help us progress towards the country's aspirational goals, which must be attained to meet the exploding aspirations of our young and talented population.

This NITI Ashtanga (eight pillars of transformative policy reforms) of India's progress towards becoming *Viksit Bharat* by 2050 are:

(i) building social capital to safeguard national unity and our celebrated diversity;
(ii) transforming governance to focus on short-term accountability and transparency;
(iii) honest acceptance of our net-zero targets and public monitoring of the progress towards achieving them;
(iv) exclusive focus on employment generation and taking jobs to where people are;
(v) using AI for attaining globally comparable standards in the quality and delivery of education and personalized health services;
(vi) reimagining private-public partnership (PPP);
(vii) achieving true strategic autonomy in our foreign policy; and

(viii) forming a coalition of the willing within the Global South comprising of Asian and African emerging economies, for redesigning global priorities such that they ensure a green and prosperous future for the global community.

A Vishwamitra Rises

To be willing to grasp the opportunities thrown up by the transitions is one thing. To be in a position to do so, however, is quite another. First and foremost, therefore, is the requirement for focused efforts to build our social capital rather than frittering it away by deepening societal cleavages due to electoral imperatives. This applies across the political spectrum. The implication is that India's much-celebrated diversity should not only be sustained but be continuously reinforced.

We have to focus on consistently strengthening our social capital by empowering the more vulnerable segments of our diverse population. Unbridled majoritarianism that is exclusionary by definition and susceptible to supremacist worldviews will erode rather than reinforce our capacity to address the challenges in the way of achieving our national goal. *Sabka Saath, Sabka Vikas, Sabka Vishwas* must apply to the entire population without any exception. It is our considered belief that stoking societal divisions—and those guilty of doing so are to be found across all communities—is inimical to improving the investment climate in the country and could also become an existential threat to our national unity and cultural and social diversity.[7] Maintaining this diversity while successfully navigating our economic transition will make India an exemplar for other nations in Asia and Africa. A true *vishwamitra*, no less.[8]

Transformation of Governance

Over 75 years after Independence, it is surely time to decisively sever our ties to the colonial governance structures which we have lived with for far too long, with evidently sub-optimal results.[9] It is now time to proactively bring all stakeholders in India's future together. A whole-of-society effort is the *sine qua non* of the country being both able and willing to negotiate the simultaneously unfolding global transitions.

Therefore, we need to quickly eliminate the present hierarchy between the government and the rest of the population comprising the private sector, the entire spectrum of entrepreneurs, academia and civil society. All stakeholders in India's future have to be on the same page and be mutually accountable. This cannot be achieved unless the colonial administrative structure is dismantled within a stipulated time frame. Several steps have, thankfully, already been taken by the present government in this direction, as in the thorough revision of the criminal procedure code and the junking of more than 1,200 laws of colonial pedigree. The Capacity Building Commission and Mission Karmayogi are also incremental steps in making governance more efficient.

But a more vigorous and bold governance reform is essential. The effort should be now to establish short-term accountability at both levels of governance leadership, political and bureaucratic. The political leadership at least submits itself to long-term accountability through the constitutionally mandated five-yearly electoral process.

The bureaucracy, however, simply has no accountability at all, except to its political masters both at the Centre and in the states, which is a fertile ground for building opaque nexuses. The colonial system of the covenanted bureaucracy being answerable only to the Viceroy, subsequently replaced by the President (and in practice to the Department of Personnel and Training in the Ministry of Home Affairs), has to be replaced by the bureaucracy becoming accountable to civil society and the taxpayers who fund their upkeep. This will require that key result indices (KRIs) be established for every member of the national covenanted services and their performance, objectively evaluated against these KRIs, be made publicly available.[10]

This system of short-term accountability can be effectively and immediately put in place at the lowest rung of administration: districts. Each of the well over 750 districts in India has on average a population of three million and a geographic area of about 4,500 square kilometres. The scale makes it eminently suitable for designing its own district development blueprint and monitoring its implementation. The blueprint must be drawn up with the active participation of all the stakeholders and not merely by some government department.

Its implementation would be monitored by a district monitoring and evaluation organization that will also have representatives from all stakeholders, viz. private businesses, academia, civil society and the administration. The modality for operationalizing short-term accountability, currently being tried as a project in a couple of states, would be to first estimate a baseline of economic and human development indicators for each district.

Using this baseline, the multi-stakeholder platform can cooperatively design the medium and annual development blueprint for each district. The district administrator, henceforth recognized as the chief executive officer for the time-bound delivery of the development blueprint, will use the targets specified in the blueprint as the relevant KRIs. Short-term mutual accountability will thus be ensured through monitoring by the multi-stakeholder platform already put in place.[11] This model when operationalized will also eliminate the 'ruler and ruled' hierarchy that currently characterizes the ground reality in the vast majority of districts in the country.[12]

Our national unity is best secured in safeguarding and strengthening the federated structure designed by our Constitution. Centralization of decision-making in Delhi is neither a guarantee for strengthening national unity, nor is it viable. Instead, states, each of them constitutionally charged with the responsibility of improving their HDIs and maintaining law and order, peace and social harmony, have to become equal partners in India's effort to navigate its way forward through the challenges.

From Pledges to Progress: The Road to Net-Zero

In his address to COP26 at Glasgow in 2021, Prime Minister Modi committed India to achieving its net-zero target by 2070, 45 years from now. This should be reflected in a decline of our per capita and total emissions. The ground reality is, however, quite different.

Our total emissions currently are 4 billion metric tons of carbon dioxide equivalent (tCO2e).[13] These emissions increased at 7 per cent in 2023 while the GDP growth was 6.7 per cent, signalling an increase in energy intensity of our GDP rather than a decline, which is the desired goal.[14] These emissions equate to 2.9 tons per capita per annum. India's emissions have been growing by 50 per cent every 10 years and are expected to peak at 14 billion tons by 2047.[15] Given that our emissions will still be rising over the next 25 years, it looks very difficult for us to achieve the net-zero target by 2070. However, India's per capita emissions were less than half the world average at 4.7 tons.[16]

We can always go back to the argument that our current per capita emissions are far below that of advanced economies and even less than half of the world average. Even cumulatively, India's share of CO2 emissions is a mere 3.7 per cent. Therefore, it can be asserted that it is both unfair and unjustified to expect

India to start reducing its emissions at this stage of its economic transition when the focus has to be achieving rapid economic growth. The underlying policy stance seems to be that while the 'drama' of these international negotiations can continue, ground realities will likely mean a further expansion of fossil-fuel-based energy generation. Another strand of this defensive argument is that with the US under the second Trump Administration now jettisoning all measures for addressing climate change, India can take cover behind this US-led disruption of global climate negotiations and continue with business as usual with some minor tweaks to thwart any overt criticism.

Before we assess the value of the above approach, it would be relevant to note that a mission on hydrogen as a source of power generation has already been established by India, which is also the originator and leader of the International Solar Alliance (ISA).

An ambitious scheme for subsidizing 10 million rooftop solar plants with the provision for absorbing their excess generation into the main national grid on a payment basis is underway. And a target for renewable energy contributing 40 per cent of total energy consumption has also been established. These are steps in the right direction which perhaps need to be better enforced to achieve the momentum required for India to reduce its carbon footprint.

For example, coal-based thermal power generation still accounts for 74 per cent of total electricity generation; the share of nuclear power has remained stagnant over the years and is only 2.7 per cent. The share of hydropower has also not increased markedly and remains at 7.7 per cent, while the share of solar and wind power in total generation has together not gone above 11.5 per cent thus far.[17]

India would do well to take seriously the warning of a rapidly closing climate change window. In addition to the dangers posed by rising sea levels, India must also take cognizance of the Asian Brown Cloud which is resulting in 30 times faster melting of the Third Pole, the Himalayas. This, in turn, poses a serious threat to the perennial nature of our mighty rivers and consequently to the agrarian economy in North India. Even a minor rise in sea levels would see a huge influx of 'climate refugees' into the country and also cause severe disruption to our own coastal clusters. India remaining in denial about climate change will be at unimaginable costs to its people and to its own national development goals. Therefore, it is imperative that in its own interest, and for the sake of the planet, the reduction of India's carbon footprint receives the highest policy attention and mission-mode implementation.

It is probable that adaptation and mitigation measures alone may no longer suffice for India to achieve its net-zero target and reduce its carbon footprint. The task at hand most likely is to remove carbon from the environment and undertake a large-scale and time-bound programme for carbon sequestration. A National Mission on Carbon Sequestration that brings together various levels of governments, multiple government agencies, and societal stakeholders ought to be established without delay. The Mission must be tasked with developing the entire range of non-fossil fuel energy-generation measures including generating energy from municipal and agricultural waste; promotion of the circular economy; encouraging energy conservation; pushing the deployment of small modular nuclear generators; and accelerating the completion of hydropower projects et al. The sooner such a multi-stakeholder Mission is established, the better.

One of the potentially most robust and effective carbon sequestration programmes can be the large-scale adoption of 'regenerative farming' that helps to reverse the ongoing decline in the organic carbon content of soil. A less noticed but devastating consequence of our nationwide adoption of biochemical-based farming with its huge dependence on chemical fertilizers, herbicides and pesticides is that our soil health has been destroyed. For any soil to remain arable, the organic carbon content has to be above 1.5 per cent. It was a healthy 2.5 per cent at the time of our Independence.[18]

Increasing quantities of chemical fertilizers dumped into farms drive out the carbon from the soil to the environment. With chemical fertilizer use increasing from 67,000 tons in the 1950s to 66.8 million tons in 2023–24, a humungous increase of 1,000 times, the organic carbon content of India's soil has declined to a shocking 0.3 per cent.

We have effectively 'desertified' our land and put our soil in the ICU. At the same time, the return on chemical fertilizers has progressively declined from 15 kilogram of grain from every additional kilogram of chemical fertilizer to less than five kilograms of grain today.[19]

Regenerative farming that does not use any chemical inputs comes in many variants. All these variants are worthy of experimentation to assess their comparative results. Anecdotal evidence from the present two million farmers who practise regenerative farming suggests all these variants result in a rise in organic carbon content of the soil. Regenerative farming also leads to several ecological benefits, such as reduced groundwater usage, enhanced release of micronutrients from the soil that directly support root health and boost yields, and lower soil temperatures. One key practice contributing to this is *achhadan*—maintaining a green cover over the soil—which helps shield it from direct sunlight and prevents excessive temperature rise.

It is important to scientifically establish the feasibility of regenerative farming for providing food and nutritional security while ensuring ecological sustainability and large-scale carbon sequestration. Once this feasibility is scientifically established,

India can lead the world in undertaking the largest carbon sequestration programme. It will also have the most impressive externality of substantially increasing farmers' incomes both by higher net revenues and earning carbon credits. Farmers' incomes will actually be doubled. The National Mission on Natural Farming (NMNF) needs to be given far more resources than the rather miserly Rs 2,500 crore allocated to it in the Budget for FY 2024–25, which is surely nugatory when compared with the allocation of Rs 2.5 lakh crore as subsidy for chemical fertilizers. This is actually a subsidy for increasing the carbon emissions from agriculture, which already accounts for 14–16 per cent of total carbon emissions in India.[20]

A Coalition of the Willing

It is quite evident that advanced economies are neither willing to accept their responsibility for violating all planetary boundaries in the past nor are they taking the required steps to save the planet from an impending environment catastrophe.

At Paris COP21 in 2015, developed countries promised to contribute $100 billion per year until 2020 and mobilize a similar amount until 2025 to help emerging economies meet the costs of climate change adaptation and mitigation measures.

This was in a way an admission of the historical truth that it is the presently advanced economies which focused exclusively on their growth with zero consideration for the global ecological system. However, until 2023, only a negligible total sum of $50 billion had been paid out by developed countries, in complete violation of their pledge.

The Paris Agreement also recognized that despite ongoing adaptation and mitigation measures (constrained by the lack of resources), some small island countries and least developed economies could suffer from severe loss and damage due to the vagaries of climate change. Therefore, a Loss and Damage (L&D) Fund—later renamed at COP29 at Baku as the Fund for Responding to Loss and Damage (FRLD)—was established at COP27 in Egypt for helping to meet the costs incurred by developing countries. It was estimated that $600 billion is required to appropriately capitalize FRLD.

At COP29, it was announced that commitments of only $720 million, one-ninth of the assessed requirement, had been received until then and disbursements would begin in 2025.[21] The unwillingness of developed countries to bear a fair burden of adaptation to and mitigation of climate change now threatens to reach the next level with the onset of the Trump 2.0 administration, which comes armed with the shocking rhetoric of 'drill, baby, drill' unleashed by the United States President.[22]

Such a stance is sure to throw a big spanner in the global efforts for preventing a catastrophic violation of planetary boundaries. This has to be resisted and provides the rationale for creating a much-needed Coalition of the Willing in the Global South.

As a consensus partner to the FRLD and itself being seriously vulnerable to vagaries of climate change, India should be seen as and become a major proponent of such a 'Coalition for Life and Saving the Planet (CLASP)'. Having already launched the ISA, which was formalized in 2020 and now has 100+ members, India is well placed to launch and operationalize CLASP.

We are not unaware, however, that history is replete with instances of rational-actor theses being upended by demagogues with short-term agendas.[23] But even if it's going to be carbon backsliding by a section of the populist political leadership in the West,[24] though it is hoped sanity will prevail, India must continue to be on the side of climate-warrior nations. There can be no succumbing to nihilism.

It is safe to say that the impending global climate catastrophe will surely be hastened if Trump's rhetoric on the issue begins reflecting in US policy. Such shortsightedness could result in fossil fuels (mainly oil, natural gas, and coal) continuing to be the largest contributors to the global energy mix, providing 75 per cent of global energy demand even in 2040 as an estimate has projected.[25] It ought to be noted that US emissions, till today, are eight times that of China and 25 times that of India; the difference is even bigger when US climate excesses are compared with, say, small island states or African nations.

India's task is thus cut out: Leverage the global transitions as a leader of the Coalition of the Willing to shape global energy demand away from fossil fuels in the coming years, thereby preventing a doomsday scenario from coming to pass.

Promoting a green economy as opposed to a hyper-consumerist economy is both in our ethos and our interest. Given India's population, geographical size, and growth projections for the years and decades ahead, adhering to such an approach which recognizes and respects planetary boundaries will make us rule-makers instead of rule-takers. India's leadership role in the Global South (where the growth is expected to come from over the coming decades) in prioritizing the transition away from carbon will be vital to discharging its responsibility to the health and wealth of its citizens, as well as benefiting the world.

Delhi will thus have to be mindful of privileging policies for clean and renewable energy and those which simultaneously secure ecological, food and nutritional security to power its growth going forward. That there cannot be a trade-off between citizens' health and welfare, and their prosperity, is a fundamental principle that must be adhered to. India should not let its choices be dictated by the fact that rich nations are reneging on climate-change funding promises or are in denial about the consequences of climate change.

Planting Jobs Where Roots Run Deep

India, with a current population of 1.42 billion, became the world's most populated country in 2024 overtaking China. Our median age at 29 years is among the lowest in the world. The working-age population will peak at 1.1 billion in 2045, when it will be 65 per cent of the total population.[26] The size of our working population will be larger than that of the US and China combined. The dependency ratio (number of children below 15 years and seniors above 65 as a ratio to the working population aged 15–64) will continue to decline until 2045. India can thus enjoy a demographic dividend for the next twenty years.

The flip side of this positive narrative is that India needs to find productive jobs for its workforce, currently estimated at about 596 million (about 60 per cent of the working-age population due to the lower female labour participation rates).[27] Without these jobs, the demographic dividend can convert to a demographic crisis with heavy human costs.

According to official statistics, labour participation rate in the country is 51 per cent. While female labour participation rate has increased somewhat sharply in recent years, it is still 37 per cent. Of the total women workforce, 18 per cent are engaged in unpaid work and nearly half are self-employed in family vocations.[28] This implies that nearly half the working-age population on average and about 70 per cent of the female working population has simply opted out of the workforce and/or stopped looking for jobs. Nearly 82 per cent of our workforce is engaged in the informal sector and 90 per cent are informally employed.[29]

Of these, 120 million are reported to be working in unincorporated sector enterprises and this number has increased by more than 10 million in 2023–24.[30] Youth employment remains at unacceptably high levels, especially for graduates. Agriculture still employs 44 per cent of workers and the transition to non-agriculture jobs seems to have stagnated and even reversed during and after the COVID pandemic years, with the share of manufacturing sector employment remaining stuck at less than 14 per cent.[31] The critical issue in terms of utilizing our demographic dividend is that nearly eight million new jobs need to be generated each year to absorb the annual additions to India's workforce. In addition, about two million new jobs are required to clear the existing backlog and accommodate the rising number of women workers as their participation rates improve.[32] Where will these jobs be generated given that AI is likely to replace large numbers of jobs in both manufacturing and services sectors?

The possible way forward is to significantly expand our labour-intensive exports. In parallel, accelerating the shift from agriculture to manufacturing is essential. This can be achieved by enhancing the overall investment climate, particularly by improving ease of doing business (EoDB) across the country. Export growth has been lower than India's GDP growth rate for the last thirty years. This is not good enough to absorb the burgeoning workforce. Our share in world merchandise trade has been stagnant at below two per cent for the past three decades. It was a mere 1.8 per cent in 2023–24. Though the share of services exports, primarily ITES (information technology enabled services), has increased and is currently 4.3 per cent of the world services trade flows, this hardly contributes to labour transition out of agriculture.[33]

One of the principal reasons for this rather lacklustre export performance could be that the central government has been seen as primarily responsible for export promotion. Given India's extensive diversity, a pan-India export promotion policy, drawn up in the Ministry of Commerce and Industry in Delhi, perhaps has negligible impact on states' export performance. The way forward could be designing state-specific export-promotion policies which take into account the comparative and competitive advantages of each state and on that basis provide effective incentives for exporters.[34] The Centre can consider assisting individual states in this effort and even monitor their progress, and incentivize good performance both fiscally and through helping with lowering the logistics cost for exporters in land-locked states like Punjab and Uttar Pradesh.

Ramping up manufactured exports has been one of the key drivers of employment generation across countries. Promoting labour-intensive manufactured exports requires significant improvement in EoDB parameters, especially for SMEs to make them vibrant partners in regional and global supply chains. The onus for improving EoDB must lie with the states. They will have to focus sharply on eliminating the regulatory and compliance burden that severely impacts our private enterprises. Prime Minister Modi announced in February 2025 the constitution of a deregulation commission to further reduce the role of the state in all spheres of governance, and rationalize the regulations/compliances which effectively strangulate private enterprise, initiative and innovation.[35] A welcome move indeed, as the regulatory and compliance burden has become a source of systemic generation of rent for the corrupt bureaucracy.

Each state government should mandate its finance minister to oversee, in as short a time as possible, the dismantling of this vicious and deadly system of regulations and compliances. It is evident over the last decade that merely digitizing the compliances and making regulations online have not served to root out the low-level bureaucratic rent seeking which reportedly is as rampant as, if not more than, it was in earlier decades.[36] Growing numbers of high-income individuals and even start-ups choosing to shift their businesses to off-shore locations is evidence (if any were needed) of the present malaise.

Service exports other than software and ITES—like cultural, education, health and tourism—are labour-intensive and have significant untapped potential. India's rank in the World Economic Forum's Travel & Tourism Development Index improved to 39 in 2024 among 119 countries, from 54 in 2021.[37] This can surely be improved further. India attracted 9.5 million foreign tourists in 2023, which is a mere 0.7 per cent of the total world tourist numbers.[38] This too can be significantly improved. Again, it will be far more effective to design state-specific tourism policies utilizing the destination management organization (DMO) model to ensure that we achieve high 'responsible tourism' levels for individual states.

Promoting SMEs, which are dispersed throughout the country, and making them globally competitive along with tourism will also effectively address another major problematic feature of India's employment situation. This concerns the large-scale internal migration that presently characterizes the Indian labour market.

Although official data is not available, it is estimated that the per-annum internal migration may be around 90 million.[39] These are the number of workers who work in locations away from their families and come home each year to temporarily unite with their families before returning to their place of work. There will be substantial welfare gains if this migration-based employment, which attracts workers to growth centres, is reversed and jobs can be generated where people actually reside. There is empirical evidence to suggest that this will bring down labour costs while improving the quality of life for the worker and her family. Given our huge social and cultural diversity, we should not seek to emulate China or Western economies where hundreds of millions of workers migrate from all over the country to growth clusters and also migrate to other countries in search of better-paid employment.

We will soon face social resistance to such large-scale migration.[40] Therefore, policy attention should be given to creating an investment-supportive environment in labour-surplus regions of Central, East and North-East India in an effort to retain labour. A mechanism to incentivize investors to move to 'aspirational districts' could be considered, as savings from higher costs of migrant labour can be used to create the conditions required to bring jobs to workers.

From Chalkboards to Code

In quantitative terms, India has made substantial progress in the education sector. We have achieved universal enrolment in primary schools. And while there is a considerable dropout rate after primary education, secondary schools absorbed 76 per cent of the student cohort in 2023.[41] [42] The gross education ratio in higher education, with its 1,100 universities and 45,000 colleges, was 28 per cent (or 43.3 million) in 2023.[43] In addition, a large number of skill-training centres have been set up under the aegis of the Pradhan Mantri Kaushal Kendra (PMKK). Apprenticeship, too, is being encouraged. After a hiatus of nearly 30 years, the government came up with the National Education Policy in 2020, which seeks to bring in much-needed flexibility and some major changes in the education system.

It is also true, however, that the quality of education being imparted does not meet the standards required to take the best advantage of our talented young population. The Annual Status of Education Report (ASER) surveys by education NGO Pratham regularly highlight the glaring weaknesses in the primary and secondary education systems. In higher education, none of the Indian universities and colleges figure in the global top 100 universities list. The ILO says nearly 40 per cent of our graduating students are unemployable. Other than IISc Bengaluru, first-generation IITs and IIMs, and a handful of others, none find a place even in the list of top 200 higher education institutions globally.

A huge effort is needed if our human capital potential is to be fully capitalized on to reap the demographic dividend. Artificial intelligence offers a very powerful instrumentality for India to take advantage of its human capital. The digitization of school education was started in September 2017 with the launch of DIKSHA (Digital Infrastructure for Knowledge Sharing) by Prime Minister Modi. We now have the prospect of putting in place the digital public intelligence infrastructure which makes available all reading and training material in the mother tongues of all our children. This will revolutionize teaching practices in primary and secondary schools.

Moreover, AI offers the tantalizing prospect of providing each student with a personalized digital teacher which can respond to their training needs. With 1.12 billion mobile phone connections, of which 900 million are smartphone subscribers, the country is poised to hugely ramp up its digital/internet network.

Already, the overall penetration rate of the internet is close to 55 per cent, representing 821 million users. By 2023, rural users at 442 million outnumbered those in urban centres.[44] This is still below the world average of 66 per cent; India must ensure universal internet availability by focusing attention on states where the internet penetration is below the national average. With the auction of 5G licences in 2022, major roll-out of 5G services by leading service providers, and rising internet penetration, the ground is now ready for an AI-backed revolution in improving the access to and quality of education across all levels.

Our education policy should now be focused on facilitating access to internet-based curricula and teaching practices both in schools and higher education institutions. In higher education, for example, the target is to raise the gross enrolment ratio (GER) from the present 28 per cent to 50 per cent by 2035, a target set by NEP 2020.[45] The increase from the present enrolment of

43.3 million students to 154 million by 2035 can only be achieved through a massive recourse to an AI-based online system of learning. Classroom-based teaching cannot possibly accomplish this target.

India has realized significant progress across all health indicators since Independence. Until 2014–15, however, the major burden for healthcare was borne privately by households, with the government only accounting for 29 per cent of gross health expenditure. The latter sought to rectify this anomaly by establishing in 2018 the National Health Authority (NHA), the apex body responsible for implementing India's flagship public health insurance/assurance scheme, Ayushman Bharat Pradhan Mantri Jan Arogya Yojana. It oversees the provision of government-paid (free) health insurance to the poorest 500 million Indians up to a value of Rs 5 lakh (approximately $6,000) annually. With the establishment of the NHA and related efforts, the government's share in health expenditure had gone up to 48 per cent in 2020–21. The scheme, now in its sixth year of operation, has 724 million members (ABHA card holders) and 475 million linked unique health records.

With the launch of the Ayushman Bharat Digital Mission (ABDM or the India Health Stack), India will create the world's largest patient-centric, interoperable and secure digital health ecosystem. As of 30 June 2024, 73.6 million hospital admissions worth Rs 1 lakh crore ($1.2 billion) have been authorized under the scheme. The Mission represents one of the best examples of the beneficial use of digital technology and provides the required platform for extensive use of AI for improving the delivery of health services. It is also urgently required as some of India's health indicators like child stunting, child malnutrition, infant mortality and female anaemia remain at worryingly high levels.[46]

Reimagining Private-Public Partnership

There is a purpose in putting 'private' ahead of 'public' in our formulation of the proposed partnership between the two sectors. For far too long, the public sector and governments at various levels have been given the lead role in forging partnerships for sectoral activities.

It is beyond argument that the Indian private sector has been the driving force for India's growth and prosperity. Even today, when the government runs big deficits, it is financed by household savings. It is accepted that the private sector in India has 25,000 tons of gold in its vaults (worth nearly $2 trillion), compared to a mere $654 billion of gold reserves with the RBI.[47] The question surely worth asking is, why should not governments at all levels actually be seen as secondary and their role be explicitly supportive of the private sector? For how much longer should we continue to live with the colonial societal framework in which government officials commandeer and the private sector dutifully obeys and performs?

It is time that this colonial structure of governance, and that which grew in the socialist decades post-Independence and took charge of the 'commanding heights of the economy', is thoroughly and quickly dismantled. We have already earlier emphasised that governments at all levels must be made accountable to the other stakeholders in the society/economy. We need now to consider measures to increase productivity and efficiency across sectors by giving a more active role to private operators, seeking to make optimal surpluses (not maximizing profits), with the government acting as the source of financial resources and as a strict supervisor which enforces the mandated contract with these private operators.

Schools, colleges, universities, hospitals, banks, airports, ports and all utilities can be managed more efficiently on the basis of this new form of private-public partnership (PPP). The supervisory role can be insulated from rent seeking by a laser-like focus on outcomes, to be judged on the basis of pre-agreed and publicly transparent key result indicators. The only sectors that will remain the exclusive monopoly of the government will be national security, law and order, contract enforcement (including role of judiciary) and external relations.

The rest can be managed with varying degrees of PPP. This will actually bring to life the maxim of 'minimum government, maximum governance'. For operationalizing this model of performance based on PPP, a degree of mutual trust between the private and public sector is essential. This will, therefore, have to start at the ground level with the village panchayats, zila parishads and district administrations, and then sequentially be raised to higher levels. However, the privatization of loss-making public sector enterprises (PSEs) belonging to both central and state governments and the monetization of their assets can proceed in parallel. Such an approach will effectively demonstrate the government's political will to limit itself to providing the essential pre-conditions for private sector-led growth and not remain in business, which in any case the government has no business to be in.

Diplomacy on Our Terms

The transition of economic heft from OECD countries to the leading nations of the Global South, especially in Asia and particularly China and India (in that order), coterminous with the geographical transition of the global centre of gravity from the transatlantic to the Indo-Pacific after a 200-odd years blip, is opening up ever newer possibilities. For India, to substantially seize these opportunities, old strategic foreign policy mindsets, which viewed geopolitics through the lens of non-alignment, will have to be jettisoned and fresh approaches to maximizing the benefits of these transitions explored.

In a world awash with transitions, strategic autonomy doesn't mean simply making choices between partners—it means having the capacity to engage with multiple partners at the same time, in ways that align with the country's long-term interests.

Locating our policy design within the above framework would include but not be limited to playing a more active role in regional trading agreements and considering the possibility of forming and leading a fourth mega trade bloc.

Reaching an accommodation with the globally rising power China in a *ceteris paribus* setting, and deepening economic as well as diplomatic engagement with the nations of the Asia/Indo-Pacific, Africa and West Asia, which are the likely future drivers of global economic growth, will also be critical. The US ought to have no objection as India will certainly continue to engage with the West on mutually beneficial terms, as liberal democracies ought to, despite their respective flaws and varied civilizational ethos. The US acceptance of India continuing to import crude oil from Russia, despite the sanctions imposed on it by Washington following the Ukrainian conflict, amply demonstrates the maturing of strategic relations between the world's two largest democracies.

We are willing to wager that there is not a single country in the Asia-Pacific, or indeed the wider Global South, which would prefer not to be squeezed by Sino-Indian competition to grow their respective strategic space—and all that it entails in the economic, security and diplomatic domains. In fact, the real 'decoupling' needed is perhaps of Sino-Indian relations from the US-India relationship. And the opportunity lies in the civilization states of China and India learning not just to live together but also to benefit from each other.

As mentioned earlier, geopolitical conflict is more accurately reflected in China-India relations than in Sino-US ties, where ideological mistrust has long shaped how Beijing and Washington perceive each other. This assessment implies that issues of contestation between China and India are, therefore, more susceptible to resolution in geopolitical terms too.

Engaging China in India's own interest is, for instance, one of the key approaches recommended in this volume to leverage the global transitions. We are entirely cognizant of the possibility that Xi and the CPC could double down on China's 'string of pearls' strategy to limit India's strategic footprint and space to grow. India's valid security and territorial concerns, though, must not make us risk-averse at this crucial juncture of the history of the world, which is pregnant with possibilities informed by the six simultaneous transitions.

In evolving a via-media which balances pitfalls and potential, the seminal intervention by Rear Admiral K. Raja Menon in his 2022 monograph *Reorienting Indian Military Grand Strategy: Defensive Territoriality to Offensive Oceanic in the Indo-Pacific*[48] defines how our punitive capability against China may be built up. But it is expressly **not** an argument for confrontation. Among the so-called security hawks, too, there is clarity that the smartest choice for India is to neither fight nor prepare to fight a two-front war.[49] Instead, India should seek a durable and enduring peace with one of its adversaries.[50]

Our argument is precisely that the unfolding impact of the global transitions could not have even been envisaged a quarter of a century ago, and therefore, India has a chance to convert its long-term strategic competition with China into a not entirely unfriendly rivalry.

The idea is not to let our guard down—by all means, Delhi should continue all that it is doing to patrol and fortify positions on the LAC as now agreed with Beijing. The security establishment must also continue to develop underwater and outer-space early warning systems, create an indigenous encryption platform, build border infrastructure, populate border villages, et al.[51] But completely ignoring or even underestimating the potentially transformative impact on India of mutually profitable economic outcomes which are possible only if accommodation can be reached with China, would not be wise.

As the lesser power, India will have to be prepared to do the initial running while it shapes domestic opinion in favour of such an approach—and China could consider a 'grand gesture' to push things along as distrust between the Asian giants runs deep. The positives could well outweigh negatives if, for example, Beijing's proven leadership and expertise in key frontier technologies is shared with Delhi, which would be massively beneficial for India to grow exponentially.

Naysayers will immediately point to the danger of tech transfer from China coming embedded with malware/spyware. The solution, however, isn't to bemoan the alleged perfidy of the Chinese but to build indigenous capacity to detect such issues and deal with them appropriately. Indeed, provided tech transfer is premised on a healthy Sino-Indian relationship based on mutual trust, access to the China market, and FDI in India, the narrative around Chinese 'sneakiness'—which is in reality plain old statecraft—will fade and eventually cease. There are umpteen historical examples of countries having been bitter enemies and then cooperating to create a win-win situation for themselves.

Similarly, perhaps against the grain, we reiterate our advocacy for India to take its rightful place as a climate-warrior nation with an ambitious domestic agenda, and in shaping the global narrative on climate-change action and financing. It is the only rational and citizen-centric way ahead and entirely in the national interest. We are obliged to ensure that the Indian people have a viable, healthy and green future—that cannot be the preserve of rich nations alone.

Strategic autonomy is, thus, not only about the ability to choose multiple partners as suited to our security needs, but also to choose the issues on which India will have the wherewithal to take its own, independent stand irrespective of the stance of other powers.

♦

We are at the end of this volume, but the tumultuous journey for India through the six simultaneously unfolding global transitions has just begun.

We must, therefore, reiterate our assessment that the end game for Pax Americana as we knew it has begun, and it will only gather pace in the years ahead. The rise of China is a *fait accompli* which India will need to understand, accept, and make peace with, challenging as the process may be. As two civilization states—and, critically, neighbours—which are home to over three billion people, a Sino-Indian compact can be the driver of prosperity, security and stability in the twenty-first century.

ACKNOWLEDGEMENTS

Our families and friends have been a source of huge support and occasional aggravation. We thank them for both!

We are deeply grateful to the veritable galaxy of thought leaders, too many to name here, who read the manuscript and offered us their incisive comments. We have tried our best to incorporate their suggestions, which have improved the book immeasurably.

Thanks are due also to our colleagues at Pahle India Foundation, especially its executive director Ravi Pokharna, for their support. A special shoutout to Yamini Chowdhury from Rupa Publications for shepherding the journey of a short essay we had written into a full-fledged volume.

Finally, the work of scholars and practitioners on the issues covered in this book remains an abiding source of knowledge and insight for us. We stand on their shoulders. All errors are, naturally, ours alone.

NOTES

Introduction

1 'Real GDP growth (Map 2025)', International Monetary Fund, https://tinyurl.com/bdhv297h. Accessed on 5 May 2025.
2 Ibid.
3 Boehm, Sophie, and Clea Schumer, '10 Big Findings from the 2023 IPCC Report on Climate Change', World Resources Institute, 20 March 2023, https://tinyurl.com/5938eyzx. Accessed on 17 April 2025.
4 These include NATO member-states not paying their share for Europe's defence, differentiated tariff regimes for less developed and developing countries as a moral and economic imperative, promotion of open markets and free trade, the US' role as the world's security guarantor, the emphasis on mitigating climate change, and others.
5 While America's European and Asian post-war allies are today in Trump's line of fire, the US seems to have conveniently forgotten that it was the assurance of an American security umbrella that set these countries on the path of focusing on rebuilding their economies while reducing spending on defence. This resulted in the establishment of an international political and economic order under Washington's leadership from which the US benefitted both during the Cold War decades and after.

Chapter 1: Pax Americana, Quo Vadis!

1 'Rapprochement with China, 1972', *Office of the Historian*, https://tinyurl.com/2xssywwe. Accessed on 17 February 2025.
2 O. Cohrs, Patrick, '"Pax Americana": the United States and the transformation of the 20th century's global', *Revista Brasileira de Política*

Internacional (RBPI), Vol. 61, No. 2, 2018, https://tinyurl.com/3nmwk8y4. Accessed on 17 February 2025.

3 Ibid.

4 'GATT/WTO', Goodson Law Library, Duke Law, https://tinyurl.com/2p8x8mu2. Accessed on 17 February 2025.

5 'The Doha Round', World Trade Organization, https://tinyurl.com/4tcz47hm. Accessed on 17 February 2025.

6 Lloyd, Richmond M., 'Creating the National Security State: A History of the Law That Transformed America', *Naval War College Review*, Vol. 63, No. 1, Winter 2010, https://tinyurl.com/yc6a4e86. Accessed on 17 February 2025. Bacevich, Andrew J. (ed.), *The Long War: A New History of U.S. National Security Policy Since World War II*, Columbia University Press, 2007.

7 NATO was followed by the Southeast Asia Treaty Organization (SEATO) and the Central Treaty Organization (CENTO). It was also the time of the Non-Aligned Movement (NAM) coming to life after the Bandung Conference of 1955. The world was thus divided into three distinct blocs—the US and its allies which were part of these treaty organizations; the Soviet Union with its allies; and NAM, which saw the coming together of countries such as China, Egypt, India and Indonesia, and subsequently grew to have 120 members.

8 Kaplan, Lawrence S., 'Western Europe in "The American Century": A Retrospective View', *Diplomatic History*, Vol. 6, No. 2, April 1982, pp. 111–24, https://tinyurl.com/4989a5uk. Accessed on 17 February 2025.

9 Krepinevich, Andrew, and Barry Watts, *The Last Warrior: Andrew Marshall and the Shaping of Modern American Defence Strategy*, Basic Books, US, 2015, passim.

10 Sargent, Daniel J., *A Superpower Transformed: The Remaking of American Foreign Relations in the 1970s*, Oxford University Press, 2015, online edition, Oxford Academic, 18 December 2014, https://tinyurl.com/4syrszn2. Accessed on 17 February 2025.

11 Seyfort, Serena, 'Explainer: What are China's "artificial islands" and why are there concerns about them', *9 News*, 26 November 2021, https://tinyurl.com/3e3vtt5h. Accessed on 17 February 2025.

12 The PLA has built military bases on these islands, including on Mischief Reef which was also claimed by longstanding US allies—the Philippines and Taiwan.

13 For example, from December 2013 to October 2015, China built artificial islands with a total area of close to 3,000 acres on seven coral reefs it occupies in the Spratly Islands in the southern part of the South

China Sea. See, Southerland, Matthew, 'China's Island Building in the South China Sea: Damage to the Marine Environment, Implications, and International Law', Staff Research Report, U.S.-China Economic and Security Review Commission, 12 April 2016, https://tinyurl.com/ybv7z75a. Accessed on 14 May 2025. Similarly, Beijing's accelerated programme of building aircraft carriers also began during this period (2013), and gained huge momentum over the next five years. See, Funaiole, Matthew P., and Bonnie S. Glaser, 'China's First Domestically Built Carrier Set to Begin Sea Trials', Centre for Strategic and International Studies, 23 April 2018, https://tinyurl.com/mt8mbefc. Accessed on 14 May 2025. Chan, Minnie, 'China speeds up building aircraft carriers but will PLA sailors be trained for hi-tech ships in time?', *South China Morning Post,* 5 January 2021, https://tinyurl.com/thaw4dhu. Accessed on 14 May 2025.

14 Schweller, Randall L., and Xiaoyu Pu, 'After Unipolarity: China's Visions of International Order in an Era of U.S. Decline', *International Security*, Vol. 36, No. 1, Summer 2011, pp. 41–72, https://tinyurl.com/3w6cbm75. Accessed on 17 February 2025.

15 Roy, Nabarun, 'Realism in the Study of International Relations in India', ORF Issue Brief, September 2018, https://tinyurl.com/v6b3srsp. Accessed on 17 February 2025.

16 'The People's Republic of China', Office of the United States Trade Representative, https://tinyurl.com/yc7buamx. Accessed on 17 February 2025.

17 Ibid.

18 According to a 2022 Goldman Sachs report, China is expected to overtake the US by 2035, but this is 10 years later than Goldman Sachs's 2011 projections. This more realistic, revised forecast reflects the twin reality of the US once again rediscovering its economic strengths, and China faced with the prospect—like Japan in the early nineties—of its growth momentum plateauing now, after having peaked.

19 Gang, Ding, 'US empire is bolstered by its military-industrial complex', *Global Times*, 22 September 2021, https://tinyurl.com/5pnh8vye. Accessed on 19 February 2025.

20 Ibid.

21 Ibid.

22 'World military expenditure reaches new record high as European spending surges', SIPRI, 24 April 2023, https://tinyurl.com/5fdnny6v. Accessed on 19 February 2025.

23 Saballa, Joe, 'China's Defense Spending "Drastically More" Than

Declared: US Admiral', *The Defense Post*, 25 April 2024, https://tinyurl.com/45nuuue4. Accessed on 17 April 2025.

24 Ibid.

25 Kersten, Alexander, Gabrielle Athanasia, and Gregory Arcuri, 'What Can Patent Data Reveal about U.S.-China Technology Competition?', CSIS, 19 September 2022, https://tinyurl.com/bdz3vtet. Accessed on 19 February 2025.

26 Kodama, Shogo, and Masaya Kato, 'China now global leader in 90% of critical tech research: think tank', *Nikkei Asia*, 29 August 2024, https://tinyurl.com/57fx3dwu. Accessed on 19 February 2025.

27 Hurst, Daniel, 'China leading US in technology race in all but a few fields, thinktank finds', *The Guardian*, 2 March 2023, https://tinyurl.com/fpcwnu36. Accessed on 19 February 2025.

28 Ibid.

29 'This week's cover', *The Economist*, 4 April 2024, https://tinyurl.com/28b7ezfs. Accessed on 19 February 2025.

30 Baskaran, Gracelin, 'Could Africa replace China as the world's source of rare earth elements?', Brookings, 29 December 2022, https://tinyurl.com/42jwfxsr. Accessed on 19 February 2025.

31 Rajghatta, Chidanand, 'China plays rare earth card as US, India dig deep', *The Times of India*, 14 April 2025, https://tinyurl.com/5n8repk6. Accessed on 5 May 2025.

32 Schmidt, B.C., and C. Wight, 'Rationalism and the "rational actor assumption" in realist international relations theory', *Journal of International Political Theory*, Vol. 19, No. 2, 2023, pp. 158–82.

33 Lungu, Andrei, 'The U.S.-China Clash Is About Ideology After All', RISAP, 7 April 2021, https://tinyurl.com/2kaeee8h. Accessed on 19 February 2025.

34 Ibid.

35 Fisher, Max, 'This 1989 speech is one of the most important in China's history—and only eight people have heard it', *Vox*, 3 June 2014, https://tinyurl.com/543u8mba. Accessed on 19 February 2025.

36 Hu, A., 'The Path to the Socialist Modernization with Chinese Characteristics', *Modernization with Chinese Characteristics and Great Power*, *Springer*, Singapore, 2023.

37 Buckle, Mark, 'Black cat, white cat...', *China Daily*, 2 August 2018, https://tinyurl.com/3p558y3v. Accessed on 19 February 2025.

38 Blattman, Christopher, *Why We Fight: The Roots of War and the Paths to Peace*, Viking, US, 2022, passim.

39 Hass, Ryan, 'A roadmap for US-China relations in 2023', Brookings, 4 January 2023, https://tinyurl.com/4p25rctz. Accessed on 19 February 2025.
40 Carlson, Tucker, 'Exclusive: Tucker Carlson Interviews Vladimir Putin', 6 February 2024, https://tinyurl.com/488w22uc. Accessed on 19 February 2025.
41 Ibid.
42 Piliavsky, Anastasia, 'Stop Putin in Ukraine. prevent WW III', *The Times of India*, 24 February 2024, https://tinyurl.com/2m5w245k. Accessed on 19 February 2025.
43 Ibid.
44 '"My cousins are killing one another": War in Ukraine splits mixed families', *Chicago Tribune*, 1 March 2022, https://tinyurl.com/5n997vw7. Accessed on 17 April 2025.
45 'China overtakes US to become India's top trading partner in FY24', *The Economic Times*, 12 May 2024, https://tinyurl.com/jzhe94tn. Accessed on 17 April 2025.
46 Raaj, Neelam, 'US-led world order is going through a big shift, and that is a good thing: Amitav Acharya', *The Times of India*, 13 April 2025, https://tinyurl.com/59x5udr3. Accessed on 5 May 2025.
47 Turchin, Peter, *End Times: Elites, Counter-Elites, and the Path of Political Disintegration*, Allen Lane, UK, 2023, pp. 260–61.
48 Ibid.
49 Jenkins, Brian Michael, 'Consequences of the War in Ukraine: The Economic Fallout', RAND, 7 March 2023, https://tinyurl.com/38cy85ph. Accessed on 21 February 2025.
50 Menon, Raja, and Rajiv Kumar, *The Long View from Delhi: To Define the Indian Grand Strategy for Foreign Policy*, Academic Foundation, Delhi, 2010, p. 75.
51 Pamuk, Humeyra, and Simon Lewis, 'US, Russia agree to restore diplomatic missions as first step in Ukraine war talks', *Reuters*, 19 February 2025, https://tinyurl.com/2p9d9nek. Accessed on 17 April 2025.
52 Sawhney, Pravin, 'MIGA or MAGA: How Modi's Haste to Please Trump May Backfire', *The Wire*, 22 February 2025, https://tinyurl.com/3mf6xsfr. Accessed on 17 April 2025.
53 Maynes, Charles, 'Putin says Russia will stop participating in its last nuclear treaty with the U.S.', *NPR*, 21 February 2023, https://tinyurl.com/3kymjuk8. Accessed on 20 February 2025.
54 Denisova, Kateryna, '"It's personal"—Why Germany still refuses to send

Taurus missiles to Ukraine', *The Kyiv Independent*, 17 September 2024, https://tinyurl.com/49sw6xbw. Accessed on 17 April 2025.

55 Sanger, David E., 'An Outburst by Trump on NATO May Push Europe to Go It Alone', *The New York Times*, 11 February 2024, https://tinyurl.com/ydv97rs2. Accessed on 20 February 2025.

56 Ibid.

57 Chenoy, Anuradha, 'Wars, Geopolitical Transitions and Paradigm Shifts', *Economic & Political Weekly*, Vol. 59, No. 4, 27 January 2024, https://tinyurl.com/yc3uhwxj. Accessed on 5 May 2025.

58 Ibid.

59 'National Security Strategy of Japan', December 2022, https://tinyurl.com/y9c6yabw. Accessed on 20 February 2025.

60 Liff, Adam P., 'No, Japan is not planning to "double its defense budget"', Brookings, 22 May 2023, https://tinyurl.com/yc6ck9sm. Accessed on 20 February 2025.

61 'Why Indonesia matters', *The Economist*, 21 March 2023, https://tinyurl.com/ye29ktuu. Accessed on 20 February 2025.

62 Ibid.

63 'Nuclearizing the Indo-Pacific', *The Jakarta Post*, 21 March 2023, https://tinyurl.com/4cme3u7h. Accessed on 21 February 2025.

64 'The United States and Indonesia Celebrate 75 Years of Diplomatic Relations', press release, U.S. Embassy Jakarta, 6 March 2024, https://tinyurl.com/38wpbhh5. Accessed on 21 February 2025.

65 Gill, Don McLain, 'Bolstering Indonesia-India strategic partnership will be mutually beneficial', *The Jakarta Post*, 2 March 2023, https://tinyurl.com/mrxwkduz. Accessed on 21 February 2025.

66 Remes, Jaana, and Homi Kharas, 'Latin America's missing middles', Brookings, 21 August 2019, https://tinyurl.com/3n94fdnj. Accessed on 21 February 2025.

67 'US to launch talks on partnership with 11 Western Hemisphere nations', *The Washington Post*, 27 January 2023, https://tinyurl.com/6p54dvt9. Accessed on 21 February 2025.

68 Studart, Rogério, 'Reimagining China-Brazil Relations Under the BRI: The Climate Imperative', CFR, https://tinyurl.com/bwxvpyzd, Accessed on 21 February 2025.

69 BRICS now has 10 members including Egypt, Ethiopia, Iran, Saudi Arabia and the United Arab Emirates.

70 Ioanes, Ellen, and Nicole Narea, 'South Africa's genocide case against Israel, explained', *Vox*, 13 January 2024, https://tinyurl.com/3t8xcku5. Accessed on 21 February 2025.

71 Gattuso, Peter, 'Did South Africa Ban American Businesses and Halt Mineral Exports to the U.S.?', *The Dispatch*, 20 February 2025, https://tinyurl.com/mrycsx6x. Accessed on 17 April 2025.
72 'Old World, Young Africa', *The New York Times*, https://tinyurl.com/3k93auhk. Accessed on 21 February 2025.
73 'National Security Strategy, 2022', The White House, Washington, https://tinyurl.com/3uu77rn. Accessed on 21 February 2025.
74 'Fact Sheet: 2022 National Defense Strategy', U.S. Department of Defense, https://tinyurl.com/ye28ndz2. Accessed on 21 February 2025.

Chapter 2: Arise, Asia

1 Lieberthal, Kenneth G., 'The American Pivot to Asia', Brookings, 21 December 2011, https://tinyurl.com/yc6bc5jk. Accessed on 16 April 2025.
2 Blackwill, Robert D., 'The U.S. Pivot to Asia and American Grand Strategy', Council on Foreign Relations, https://tinyurl.com/386vkph8. Accessed on 16 April 2025.
3 Ibid.
4 Ibid.
5 Blackwill, Robert D., and Richard Fontaine, *Lost Decade*, Oxford University Press, New York, 2024.
6 'Maddison Historical Statistics', University of Groningen, https://tinyurl.com/yk6mxzs7. Accessed on 16 April 2025. 'Share of world GDP throughout history', *Infogram*, https://tinyurl.com/2s3nardt. Accessed on 16 April 2025.
7 'Big Era Seven: Landscape Unit 7.1', *World History for Us All*, https://tinyurl.com/4pyhkwu8. Accessed on 16 April 2025.
8 'Share of world GDP throughout history', *Infogram*, https://tinyurl.com/2s3nardt. Accessed on 16 April 2025.
9 Maddison, Angus, 'The World Economy: A Millennial Perspective', Development Centre Studies, OECD, https://tinyurl.com/4uvd6w2r. Accessed on 17 April 2025.
10 Mainardi, Benjamin, 'Remembering the Geography in Geopolitics and Indo-Pacific Discourse', The Strategy Bridge, 7 July 2021, https://tinyurl.com/2p8mdmc3. Accessed on 16 April 2025.
11 Ibid.
12 'Geopolitics, Geoeconomics and International Order', Friedrich Ebert Stiftung, https://tinyurl.com/3dpbt5er. Accessed on 16 April 2025.
13 'Map of the geopolitical competition in the Indo-Pacific', Friedrich Ebert Stiftung, https://tinyurl.com/wnrxvckc. Accessed on 16 April 2025.

14 Mainardi, Benjamin, 'Remembering the Geography in Geopolitics and Indo-Pacific Discourse', The Strategy Bridge, 7 July 2021, https://tinyurl.com/2p8mdmc3. Accessed on 16 April 2025.

15 Russian foreign minister Sergey Lavrov, in May 2025, reignited the Indo-Pacific versus Asia-Pacific debate with a series of blunt remarks about the West's intentions against China by using India. He said that the 'Indo-Pacific region never existed…it was made up (by the US-led West) to drag India into anti-China schemes'. See, '"Indo-Pacific Region Never Existed, Made Up to Drag India Into Anti-China Schemes": Russian FM Lavrov', *The Wire*, 31 May 2025, https://tinyurl.com/2r74d7va. Accessed on 3 June 2025.

16 Evans, Gareth, 'Asian Geopolitics in transition', Asia Society, https://tinyurl.com/4shhube4. Accessed on 16 April 2025.

17 Ibid.

18 Poon, Jessie P.H., et.al., 'End of the Asia-Pacific: Geoeconomics, belt and road and the Indo-Pacific', *Political Geography*, Vol. 108, January 2024, https://tinyurl.com/mvsfjw6a. Accessed on 16 April 2025.

19 Ibid.

20 Ibid.

21 Ibid.

22 Chenglong, Jiang, 'Indo-Pacific strategy aims to maintain US hegemony', *China Daily*, 1 June 2024, https://tinyurl.com/2jy5u39t. Accessed on 16 April 2025.

23 Sachdeva, Gulshan, 'India's Reluctant Participation in the Evolving Indo-Pacific Economic Architecture', The National Bureau of Asian Research, 9 November 2023, https://tinyurl.com/55mnykjv. Accessed on 16 April 2025.

24 See Chapter 3, 'Geoeconomic Transition', in this volume for a discussion on the options for India in a post spaghetti-bowl world of mega trading blocs.

25 Sachdeva, Gulshan, 'India's Reluctant Participation in the Evolving Indo-Pacific Economic Architecture', The National Bureau of Asian Research, 9 November 2023, https://tinyurl.com/55mnykjv. Accessed on 16 April 2025.

26 Ibid.

Chapter 3: Imagine There's No Heaven

1 MAGA has twin objectives—to restore America's manufacturing prowess under the tariff wall, and reclaim the US' unipolar global position based

on hard power. See Sheng, Andrew, 'What Trump really wants is to be rid of a "loser war" in Ukraine', *South China Morning Post*, 14 March 2025, https://tinyurl.com/yus8f3uu. Accessed on 17 April 2025.

2 Williamson, John, 'A Short History of the Washington Consensus', *Law and Business Review of the Americas*, 2009, https://tinyurl.com/4th7jat3. Accessed on 27 February 2025.

3 Rajesh, Shivani, 'FTA and the WTO Regime–Explaining the Spaghetti Bowl Effect', *CMR University Journal*, Vol. 5, No. 2, August 2023, https://tinyurl.com/bd4xwc66. Accessed on 27 February 2025.

4 Maddison, Angus, 'The World Economy: A Millennial Perspective', Development Centre Studies, https://tinyurl.com/4uvd6w2r. Accessed on 27 February 2025.

5 'Experts explore potential of global transition to circular economy', Department of Economic and Social Affairs', United Nations, https://tinyurl.com/mrxzjpcj. Accessed on 27 February 2025.

6 Ibid.

7 Freidman, Thomas, *The World Is Flat*, Penguin, US, 2005, passim.

8 Gilbert, Marc, et al., 'Protectionism, Pandemic, War, and the Future of Trade', BCG, January 2023, https://tinyurl.com/2ks42584. Accessed on 27 February 2025.

9 'The Inflation Reduction Act: Here's what's in it', McKinsey and Company, 24 October 2024, https://tinyurl.com/m7ja8u2d. Accessed on 27 February 2024.

10 Goldman Sachs, *The Path to 2075—Slower Global Growth, But Convergence Remains Intact*, 6 December 2022, https://tinyurl.com/3bmhd2hr. Accessed on 27 February 2025.

11 'Slowbalisation: The future of global commerce', *The Economist*, 26 January 2019, https://tinyurl.com/3hd7bbj9. Accessed on 17 April 2025.

12 'Globalization in transition: The future of trade and value chains', McKinsey Global Institute, 16 January 2019, https://tinyurl.com/wj2w347h. Accessed on 27 February 2025.

13 Troyjo, Marcos, 'Globalisation in transition', Central Banking, 27 May 2021, https://tinyurl.com/37uz3xnn. Accessed on 27 February 2025.

14 Ibid. Troyjo proceeds to try and provide an answer to the question he raises, saying that while there is no clear vision of what the world will look like in the future, three aspects should be noted.

15 As economist Amita Batra formulates the question: 'Who will India trade with?'

16 Nan, Zhong, 'Nation to grant FDI greater access to its markets', *China*

Daily, 19 March 2024, https://tinyurl.com/25uaaxpd. Accessed on 27 February 2025.

17 Ibid.

18 Troyjo, Marcos, 'Globalisation in transition', *centralbanking.com*, 27 May 2021, https://tinyurl.com/37uz3xnn. Accessed on 17 April 2025.

19 Porter, Michael E., 'The Competitive Advantage of Nations', *Harvard Business Review*, March–April 1990, https://tinyurl.com/58txsjjy. Accessed on 27 February 2025.

20 'Despite job losses, lower prices from trade with China have left US households massively better off', *LSE Blogs*, 14 August 2019, https://tinyurl.com/5n7mwvnv. Accessed on 27 February 2025.

21 According to UN Comtrade Observatory of Economic Complexity figures quoted by the US-based Council on Foreign Relations, goods imported by the US from China in 2021 included electronics worth over $120 billion, machinery and appliances worth $120 billion, toys and games to the value of $40 billion, and between $40 billion and $20 billion each of textiles, plastics and rubbers, metals, furniture, and chemical products.

22 Hamilton, Daniel S., 'Who is America's top commercial partner? (Hint: It's not China.)', Brookings, 21 March 2024, https://tinyurl.com/bdfujunc. Accessed on 27 February 2025.

23 Ibid.

24 Ibid.

25 Hass, Ryan, 'The "new normal" in US-China relations: Hardening competition and deep interdependence', Brookings, 12 August 2021, https://tinyurl.com/yc6mnmzb. Accessed on 27 February 2025.

26 Varley, Kevin, 'US reshoring of supply chain to be limited by costs, studies say', *The Economic Times*, 14 January 2023, https://tinyurl.com/452r4rjy. Accessed on 27 February 2025.

27 Lubin, David, 'Why a more inward-looking China is bad news for the world economy', Chatman House, 17 October 2022, https://tinyurl.com/mhdnncef. Accessed on 28 February 2025.

28 'Table of total value of imports and exports (in US dollars) A: Annual table', General Administration of Customs of the People's Republic of China, https://tinyurl.com/yufsy6am. Accessed on 17 April 2025.

29 'China reports current account surplus in 2023', *Xinhua*, 18 February 2024, https://tinyurl.com/43c9pd66. Accessed on 28 February 2025.

30 Desheng, Cao, Liu Zhihua, and Fan Feifei, 'Nation to further expand opening-up, premier says', *China Daily*, 24 March 2024, https://tinyurl.com/47aevh5j. Accessed on 28 February 2025.

31 Ibid.

32 'Reassessing the role of State Ownership in China's Economy', SCCEI China Briefs, Stanford Center on China's Economy and Institutions, 15 January 2024, https://tinyurl.com/yun2msuu. Accessed on 28 February 2025.
33 Ibid.
34 Ibid.
35 Ibid.
36 Ibid.
37 Green, Mark A., 'Debt Distress on the Road to "Belt and Road"', *Stubborn Things*, Wilson Center, 16 January 2024, https://tinyurl.com/36sstc8a. Accessed on 28 February 2025.
38 Schuman, Michael, 'China's Inexorable Rise to Superpower Is History Repeating Itself', *Bloomberg*, 27 October 2020, https://tinyurl.com/254syun7. Accessed on 28 February 2025.
39 Kharpal, Arjun, 'In battle with U.S., China to focus on 7 "frontier" technologies from chips to brain-computer fusion', *CNBC*, 5 March 2021, https://tinyurl.com/j85ca898. Accessed on 28 February 2025.
40 'ASPI's Critical Technology Tracker finds China ahead in 37 of 44 technologies evaluated', *IEEE ComSoc Technology Blog*, 3 March 2023, https://tinyurl.com/3mk43eev. Accessed on 28 February 2025.
41 Tan, Weizhen, 'China's aging population will be a "big shock" to the global supply chain, says economist', *CNBC*, 12 May 2021, https://tinyurl.com/yeyx57xm. Accessed on 28 February 2025.
42 'How Severe Are China's Demographic Challenges?', *China Power*, https://tinyurl.com/bdf2w6jr. Accessed on 28 February 2025.
43 Siqi, Ji, 'China GDP: avoiding "middle-income trap" is key in 2023, and 5 per cent economic growth possible, Beijing adviser says', *South China Morning Post*, 24 November 2022, https://tinyurl.com/35uk5p4y. Accessed on 28 February 2025.
44 Zhao, Wei, 'What is Capitalism with Chinese Characteristics', April 2015, https://tinyurl.com/2rtwcve8. Accessed on 16 May 2025.
45 Ibid.
46 'United States', World Bank Group, https://tinyurl.com/55xawhk4. Accessed on 28 February 2025.
47 'GDP per capita, PPP (constant 2021 international $) - United States', World Bank Group, https://tinyurl.com/4z766ndt. Accessed on 28 February 2025.
48 'The Path to 2075—Slower Global Growth, But Convergence Remains Intact', Goldman Sachs, 6 December 2022, https://tinyurl.com/3bmhd2hr. Accessed on 17 April 2025.

49 'Moderating Inflation and Steady Growth Open Path to Soft Landing 2024', World Economic Outlook Update, January 2024, https://tinyurl.com/mer537nw. Accessed on 28 February 2025.

50 Ibid.

51 Ibid.

52 Sheng, Andrew, 'A global state of disunion', *Philippine Daily Inquirer*, 28 March 2024, https://tinyurl.com/mr23uu2r. Accessed on 28 February 2024.

53 Ibid.

54 Ibid.

55 Venu, M.K., 'On Trump's Capitulation and Why Jaishankar Should Be Careful Before Pledging Allegiance', *The Wire*, 11 April 2025, https://tinyurl.com/48xfapaj. Accessed on 7 May 2025.

56 Brooks, Robin, 'Key themes at the IMF/World Bank Spring Meetings: Dollar dominance', Brookings, 25 April 2024, https://tinyurl.com/9whderw6. Accessed on 28 February 2025.

57 Ibid.

58 There is even talk of the Plaza Accord of 1985 being repeated under a putative 'Mar-a Lago Accord'. In 1986, all G7 countries agreed to an orderly weakening of the dollar which had strengthened by 50 per cent over the previous five years. Today, however, China is a major player, and may resist such an arrangement as Beijing looks to push its exports to raise its own slackening economic growth.

59 Uchitelle, Louis, 'The U.S. Still Leans on the Military-Industrial Complex', *The New York Times*, 22 September 2017, https://tinyurl.com/yu99fbtz. Accessed on 28 February 2025.

60 'US Defense Industry Size & Share Analysis - Growth Trends & Forecasts (2025–2030)', Mordor Intelligence, https://tinyurl.com/2dsumefr. Accessed on 28 February 2025.

61 'The U.S. Defense Industry and Arms Sales', *Stanford.edu*, https://tinyurl.com/mubuzzue. Accessed on 28 February 2025.

62 Tariff hikes for Mexico, Canada and China, and on all imports of steel and aluminium have already been announced by the Trump 2.0 administration by March 2025. A slew of other tariff increases, reciprocal and otherwise, are also slated to come into force. MAGA is apparently premised upon reviving and expanding US manufacturing capacities at any cost.

63 Hamilton, Daniel S., 'Who is America's top commercial partner? (Hint: It's not China.)', Brookings, 21 March 2024, https://tinyurl.com/bdfujunc. Accessed on 28 February 2025.

64 Ibid.

65 Baldwin, Richard, 'Globalization isn't dead, it's transforming – and that will change how we do business', IMD, 26 June 2023, https://tinyurl.com/bdhdytnd. Accessed on 28 February 2025.

66 'India, EFTA's historic free trade agreement has a $100 billion investment plan', *Hindustan Times*, 10 March 2024, https://tinyurl.com/4reea6ct. Accessed on 28 February 2025.

67 'Electronics exports soar 28% in Apr-Nov of FY25, led by smartphone surge', IBEF, 26 December 2024, https://tinyurl.com/bddh87kw. Accessed on 17 April 2025.

68 It will also help if the MEA increased the number of Desks covering Africa from two (inadequate) Desks at present to at least four; each Desk, usually headed by a joint secretary, will still be dealing with more than ten countries, on average.

69 The sanctioned strength of Indian Foreign Service officers is 1,177. See 'QUESTION NO- 3468 POSTING OF INDIAN DIPLOMATS', Ministry of External Affairs, Government of India, 21 March 2025, https://tinyurl.com/2ec4ajhp. Accessed on 17 April 2025.

70 A good beginning has been made with the setting up of a specialist China cell within the MEA under the leadership of a retired senior armed forces officer, and staffed by a clutch of language and sector specialists.

71 '"A foreign policy for Viksit Bharat": Jaishankar decodes why India must revamp its diplomatic approach', *The Economic Times*, 15 December 2024, https://tinyurl.com/mubzuujh. Accessed on 7 May 2025.

72 For example, the government of Australia merged its Department of Trade and Customs into its Department of External Affairs as early as 1987. It is now known as the Department of Foreign Affairs and Trade (DFAT). This seems entirely logical in the context of the primacy of economic relations in both bilateral ties and in multilateral fora. See 'Our History', Department of Foreign Affairs and Trade, Australian Government, 24 January 2013, https://tinyurl.com/mnjfa8w4. Accessed on 17 April 2025.

73 TAN, CK, 'China sets GDP growth target of "around 5%" for 2024', *Nikkei Asia*, 5 March 2024, https://tinyurl.com/2vauw9bw. Accessed on 28 February 2025.

Chapter 4: Shifting Clout

1 'Data is the new gold. This is how it can benefit everyone – while harming no one', World Economic Forum, 29 July 2020, https://tinyurl.com/2s4awnpz. Accessed on 7 May 2025.

2 Ibid.

3 'Marcos Troyjo: How Should Government and Economics Respond to the Changing Contours of Globalization?', ACCEPT, https://tinyurl.com/5dxpxwfd. Accessed on 15 April 2025.

4 'Economic power shift', University of Sydney, https://tinyurl.com/ynptcfse. Accessed on 15 April 2025.

5 'The GDP Of BRICS Countries Surpasses $31 Trillion in 2025', *Economics Insider*, 13 March 2025, https://tinyurl.com/3phbpzuw. Accessed on 17 April 2025.

6 'Regional Comprehensive Economic Partnership (RCEP) – what it means for international trade', *Customs and Trade News*, November 2020, https://tinyurl.com/3mfv6j4j. Accessed on 15 April 2025.

7 'GDP (current US$) - European Union', World Bank Group, https://tinyurl.com/nh9svfcm. Accessed on 15 April 2025.

8 'Population, total –European Union', World Bank Group, https://tinyurl.com/2m67amjd. Accessed on 15 April 2025.

9 Suruga, Tsubasa, 'Thailand, Malaysia see strong export rebound on tech upcycle', *Nikkei Asia*, 30 August 2024, https://tinyurl.com/ycxtpwa9. Accessed on 15 April 2025.

10 Nayyar, Deepak, *Resurgent Asia: Diversity in Development*, Oxford University Press, 2019, online edition, Oxford Academic. Accessed on 15 April 2025.

11 'Economic power shift', University of Sydney, https://tinyurl.com/ynptcfse. Accessed on 15 April 2025.

12 Saul, Derek, 'China And India Will Overtake U.S. Economically By 2075, Goldman Sachs Economists Say', *Forbes*, 6 December 2022, https://tinyurl.com/ms58dx9h. Accessed on 15 April 2025.

13 Mahbubani, Kishore, 'Measuring the power of the Global South', Chatman House, 2 February 2024, https://tinyurl.com/bdfebp99. Accessed on 15 April 2025.

14 'Economic power shift', University of Sydney, https://tinyurl.com/ynptcfse. Accessed on 15 April 2025.

15 Sheng, Andrew, 'Can AI unlock productivity and growth?', *The Jakarta Post*, 18 June 2024, https://tinyurl.com/2wu6keah. Accessed on 15 April 2025.

16 European Round Table for Industry, *ERT 2024 Benchmarking Report*, 2024, https://tinyurl.com/yz6yemct. Accessed on 15 April 2025.
17 'An ice-bath for EU leaders. Competitiveness is crumbling: Europe's business case needs a rebuild', European Round Table for Industry, 18 March 2024, https://tinyurl.com/4neavwr7. Accessed on 15 April 2025.
18 Sheng, Andrew, 'Can AI unlock productivity and growth?', *The Jakarta Post*, 18 June 2024, https://tinyurl.com/2wu6keah. Accessed on 15 April 2025.
19 'The World in 2050', PwC, https://tinyurl.com/249vswru. Accessed on 15 April 2025.
20 Nayyar, Deepak, *Resurgent Asia: Diversity in Development*, Oxford University Press, 2019, online edition, Oxford Academic. Accessed on 15 April 2025.
21 Ibid.
22 Ibid.
23 Zhou, Cissy, 'Chinese investment in Asia rose 37% in 2023, led by Indonesia', *Nikkei Asia*, 7 March 2024, https://tinyurl.com/89w32v5f. Accessed on 15 April 2025.
24 Ibid.
25 Sheng, Andrew, 'Should finance lead the real sector?', *The Star*, 1 June 2024, https://tinyurl.com/3va8x5cf. Accessed on 15 April 2025.
26 Ibid.
27 Jie, Zhang, 'India's Strengthening Relationship with the Global South: Strategic Ambitions and Constraints', CSIS, 15 January 2024, https://tinyurl.com/dynejjyh. Accessed on 15 April 2025.
28 Ibid.
29 Sarkar, D., *Echoes of the Global South: Geoeconomic Power Shifts for a New Global Order*, Centre of Geoeconomics for the Global South (COGGS), Dubai, 2024.
30 'Chinese companies are winning the global south', *The Economist*, 1 August 2024, https://tinyurl.com/4d8yth8h. Accessed on 15 April 2025.
31 Rinaldi, Patrícia Nogueira, 'The Vital Role of South-South Cooperation and Its Importance for the Summit of the Future', Global Governance Forum, 12 August 2023, https://tinyurl.com/yyedn29p. Accessed on 15 April 2025.
32 'Policy Briefs', United Nations, https://tinyurl.com/365uhrat. Accessed on 15 April 2025.
33 Chinoy, Sujan, 'Why India's efforts to engage Global South is a forceful idea', *Firstpost*, 10 December 2024, https://tinyurl.com/53rudb8s. Accessed on 7 May 2025.

34 'India, China should implement Modi-Xi "important consensus" to improve ties: Chinese FM Wang tells Jaishankar', *The Economic Times*, 19 November 2024, https://tinyurl.com/47a7dmk3. Accessed on 7 May 2025.

35 In April 2025, against the backdrop of the Trump-initiated tariff wars, Beijing reached out to Delhi. The Chinese envoy to India Ambassador Xu Feihong said his country was ready to welcome imports of more premium Indian goods, and help Indian businesses tap into the Chinese market demands to address India's trade deficit that had reportedly widened to a record $99.2 billion. He also expressed the hope that India would provide a 'transparent and non-discriminatory' business environment for Chinese companies. See Parashar, Sachin, 'As trade deficit mounts, China says ready to import more premium goods from India; Envoy seeks fair environment for Chinese firms', *The Times of India,* 19 April 2025, https://tinyurl.com/4fuj6acd. Accessed on 7 May 2025.

Chapter 5: The Golden Mean

1. 'The Life of Dolly', The Roslin Institute, University of Edinburgh, https://tinyurl.com/587ym3db. Accessed on 4 April 2025.

2 Chomsky, Noam, 'The False Promise of ChatGPT', *The New York Times*, 8 March 2023, https://tinyurl.com/yypvkmjx. Accessed on 4 April 2025.

3 West, Darrell M., and John R. Allen, 'How artificial intelligence is transforming the world', Brookings, 24 April 2018, https://tinyurl.com/28mcskhc. Accessed on 4 April 2025.

4 Hu, Charlotte, and Amanda Downie, 'What is sentient AI?', IBM, 30 December 2024, https://tinyurl.com/5ydnwz6x. Accessed on 4 April 2025.

5 Pillay, Tharin, 'Amandeep Singh Gill: United Nations Secretary-General's Envoy on Technology', *Time*, 5 September 2024, https://tinyurl.com/29778v3c. Accessed on 4 April 2025.

6 Villasenor, John, 'Can AI systems create trade secrets that no human is aware of?', Brookings, 11 July 2024, https://tinyurl.com/2fpxtam3. Accessed on 26 May 2025.

7 Murgia, Madhumita, *Code Dependent: Living in the Shadow of AI*, Picador India, 2024, passim.

8 Shimizu, Kosuke, and Kazuyuki Okudaira, '"Godfather of AI" speaks on threat of tech surpassing humanity', *Nikkei Asia*, 31 March 2024, https://tinyurl.com/2kmmpr5v. Accessed on 4 April 2025.

9 @elonmusk, *X* (formerly Twitter), 15 June 2024, 7.24 p.m., https://tinyurl.com/2cxyvhaw. Accessed on 4 April 2025.

10 Ibid.

11 'Is Xi Jinping an AI doomer?', *The Economist*, 25 August 2024, https://tinyurl.com/33wdp83z. Accessed on 4 April 2025.

12 Burns, J. H., 'Happiness and Utility: Jeremy Bentham's Equation', *Utilitas*, Vol. 17, No. 1, 2005, pp. 46–61, https://tinyurl.com/ah63np8h. Accessed on 4 April 2025.

13 Somers, Meredith, 'How generative AI can boost highly skilled workers' productivity', MIT Sloan School of Management, 19 October 2023, https://tinyurl.com/bdfcrz67. Accessed on 7 May 2025.

14 'Artificial intelligence in education', UNESCO, https://tinyurl.com/2e724t7c. Accessed on 7 May 2025.

15 A very good example is the amount of royalty paid each year by Suzuki India—established as Maruti India with 74 per cent of its equity owned by the government of India, which was subsequently bought out by Suzuki Japan to make the Indian entity a fully owned subsidiary of the Japanese parent company—to its parent company in Japan. Annual royalty payments between 2020 and 2023 were estimated to be ₹142.65 billion. Total royalty payments made by the company since the start of its operations in the mid-1980s are estimated to be between ₹55,000 crore and ₹60,000 crore.

16 The Korean example in support of this caveat is a telling one. A Korean company was negotiating with Dow Chemicals for transfer of technology. Dow was insisting on a set of very tough conditions, which were unacceptable to the Korean company. The Korean company commissioned the Korea Advanced Institute of Science and Technology (KAIST) to develop a domestic alternative. KAIST successfully developed the alternative, but by that time, Dow, realizing the advances being made by KAIST, agreed to substantially dilute the terms of technology transfer. The Korean company then acquired the proven Dow technology. However, KAIST benefited significantly as it developed the capacity and expertise in the field of polymer technology which then allowed it work with other start-ups to launch other products.

17 'Defence imports decline by Rs 10,990 crore in 2014-15', *The Economic Times*, 11 July 2018, https://tinyurl.com/bdfy3np5. Accessed on 17 April 2025.

18 PIB, 'New Procurement Policy', Ministry of Defence, 4 April 2022, https://tinyurl.com/yh58aavj. Accessed on 4 April 2025.

19 PTI, 'Defence procurement from foreign sources reducing, shows govt

data', *Business Standard*, 13 March 2023, https://tinyurl.com/28xcr7hh. Accessed on 4 April 2025.

20 PIB, 'Record 75 per cent of defence capital procurement budget earmarked for domestic industry in FY 2023-24, announces Raksha Mantri at 14th Aero India', Ministry of Defence, 15 February 2023, https://tinyurl.com/5n7tcuk5. Accessed on 4 April 2025.

21 The Centre of Excellence in Biotechnology was established in the Institute of Chemical Technology, Mumbai. Similarly, the Polymer Science and Engineering Division was set up at the National Chemical Laboratory in Pune.

22 Among the various schemes which are already in place are the Emeritus Scientist Scheme, CSIR-Nehru Science Postdoctoral Research Fellowship Scheme, and CSIR Sponsored Research Grants. See 'CSIR – HRDG', CSIR, https://tinyurl.com/nynmba5z. Accessed on 4 April 2025.

23 'India's R&D investment lags behind global peers, private sector involvement low: Economic Survey', *The Economic Times*, 22 July 2024, https://tinyurl.com/ym92n23p. Accessed on 4 April 2025.

24 Walia, Aggam, '"Urgent need to reimagine India's R&D strategy": NITI Aayog paper draws lessons from China', *The Indian Express*, 7 April 2025, https://tinyurl.com/328b7ryx. Accessed on 17 April 2025.

25 'U.S. R&D Totaled $892 Billion in 2022; Estimate for 2023 Indicates Further Increase to $940 Billion', National Center for Science and Engineering Statistics, 27 February 2025, https://tinyurl.com/4zsjaps2. Accessed on 17 April 2025.

26 'India's R&D investment lags behind global peers, private sector involvement low: Economic Survey', *The Economic Times*, 22 July 2024, https://tinyurl.com/ym92n23p. Accessed on 4 April 2025.

27 iSPIRT co-founder Sharad Sharma has consistently argued that India urgently requires homegrown protocols which promote coherence between tech architecture, market architecture, and regulatory architecture to reap the benefits of data economy in the AI economy of the future.

28 During his Independence Day address in 2021, PM Modi mentioned that there were more than 60,000 regulatory compliances which the private sector faced in its routine operations. He also assured action on eliminating these, and about 1,200 have since been jettisoned. The government has also decriminalized compliances so that they no longer carry penal (prison) sentences.

29 Verma, Anoop, 'Bhashini: The fundamental driver of linguistic empowerment, social inclusion & economic progress', *ET Government*,

23 September 2024, https://tinyurl.com/374wkbtb. Accessed on 4 April 2025.

30 Constantz, Jo, and Alicia Tang, 'US Dockworkers Strike to Stop Automation Already Seen at Other Ports', *Bloomberg*, 1 October 2024, https://tinyurl.com/cpb56ar2. Accessed on 4 April 2025.

31 Chaturvedi, Aditya, 'Balance of Innovation key to Balance of Power, says Parag Khanna', *Geospatial World*, 25 January 2022, https://tinyurl.com/2sbe6k7p. Accessed on 4 April 2025.

32 Leung, Jennifer Wong, et al., 'ASPI's two-decade Critical Technology Tracker', Australian Strategic Policy Institute, https://tinyurl.com/mrxk7cry. Accessed on 4 April 2025.

33 Dutta, Amrita Nayak, 'Here's how India secured 80% jet engine tech transfer from GE Aerospace', *The Indian Express*, 24 June 2023, https://tinyurl.com/srmfz8y3. Accessed on 4 April 2025.

34 'India - U.S. Joint Statement (February 13, 2025)', Ministry of External Affairs, Government of India, 13 February 2025, https://tinyurl.com/wn82rhks. Accessed on 7 May 2025.

35 Sawhney, Pravin, 'MIGA or MAGA: How Modi's Haste to Please Trump May Backfire', *The Wire*, 22 February 2025, https://tinyurl.com/3mf6xsfr. Accessed on 7 May 2025.

36 Chaturvedi, Aditya, 'Balance of Innovation key to Balance of Power, says Parag Khanna', *Geospatial World*, 25 January 2022, https://tinyurl.com/2sbe6k7p. Accessed on 4 April 2025.

37 Hass, Ryan, 'The "new normal" in US-China relations: Hardening competition and deep interdependence', Brookings, 12 August 2021, https://tinyurl.com/yc6mnmzb. Accessed on 4 April 2025.

38 'Sizing the prize', PwC, https://tinyurl.com/ytaws8af. Accessed on 4 April 2025.

39 'Exploring new regions: The greenfield opportunity in semiconductors', McKinsey & Company, 29 January 2024, https://tinyurl.com/5cbzjbkp. Accessed on 4 April 2025.

40 Tuteja, Akhilesh, 'Semiconductor: The new driver of geopolitical balance, economic growth', *Business Standard*, 4 January 2024, https://tinyurl.com/52du7zef. Accessed on 4 April 2025.

41 Si, Ma, 'Chinese chip association opposes the reported US, Dutch, Japan deal', *China Daily*, 15 February 2023, https://tinyurl.com/2k7nhe5m. Accessed on 4 April 2025.

42 Kullab, Samya, Hanna Arhirova, and Aamer Madhani, 'US and Ukraine sign deal giving US access to country's valuable mineral wealth', Associated Press, https://tinyurl.com/rumypv6e. Accessed on 7 May 2025.

43 Chaudhury, Dipanjan Roy, 'Africa pushes back against China's predatory practices in rare earth mineral sector', *The Economic Times*, 18 September 2023, https://tinyurl.com/3638w28c. Accessed on 4 April 2025.

44 Wheeler, Tom, 'Licensing AI is not the answer—but it contains the answers', Brookings, 12 February 2024, https://tinyurl.com/4mvt8ckz. Accessed on 4 April 2025.

45 Ibid.

46 Mashelkar, R.A., and Ravi Pandit, *Leapfrogging to Pole-vaulting: Creating the Magic of Radical yet Sustainable Transformation*, Viking India, 2018, passim.

47 'Time100 AI 2024', *Time*, https://tinyurl.com/3dc69ntw. Accessed on 4 April 2025.

Chapter 6: Climate Conundrum

1 Ritchie, Hannah, et al., 'Greenhouse gas emissions', *Our World in Data*, https://tinyurl.com/3sk43v3c. Accessed on 10 April 2025.

2 Greenfield, Emily, 'Global Carbon Emissions: Country-by-Country for 2023', *SigmaEarth*, 11 November 2023, https://tinyurl.com/2p7p729f. Accessed on 10 April 2025.

3 'Scaling up Climate Finance for Emerging Markets and Developing Economies', Speech by Deputy Managing Director Bo Li at EIB Group Forum 2023, 27 February 2023, https://tinyurl.com/5348wkun. Accessed on 10 April 2025.

4 Mohan, Vishwa, 'Require 42% cut in annual carbon emissions by 2030, says UNEP', *The Times of India*, 25 October 2024, https://tinyurl.com/34swsuxp. Accessed on 10 April 2025.

5 'The economics of climate change: no action not an option', Swiss Re Institute, April 2021, https://tinyurl.com/yh6xapnm. Accessed on 10 April 2025.

6 Gupte, Eklavya, 'Renewables set for rapid long-term growth as role of hydrocarbons declines: BP', S&P Global, 30 January 2023, https://tinyurl.com/yc836uc6. Accessed on 10 April 2025.

7 Ibid.

8 Ibid.

9 International Energy Agency, *World Energy Outlook 2022*, https://tinyurl.com/2ejn8h9n. Accessed on 10 April 2025.

10 'Global Energy Market Outlook Hydrocarbon demand', Government of Alberta, September 2018, https://tinyurl.com/2kjn7myd. Accessed on 10 April 2025.

11 As almost universally expected, COP29 ended dismally with not even a sign of an agreement on the means to mobilize the required amount of $1 trillion each year for financing the adaptation and mitigation measures essential to keep poor economies afloat in the face of rising environment damages.

12 Jain, Megha, and Vanyaa Gupta, 'COP29: A ditch in the green aspirations of developing countries', *ET Government*, 4 December 2024, https://tinyurl.com/59u6recr. Accessed on 10 April 2025.

13 Blondeel, Mathieu, et al., 'Global energy scenarios: A geopolitical reality check', *Global Environmental Change,* Vol. 84, January 2024, https://tinyurl.com/4x8vx8ne. Accessed on 10 April 2025.

14 Ibid.

15 Ibid.

16 Song, Sha, 'Funding the green technology innovation pipeline: Lessons from China', World Economic Forum, 8 May 2024, https://tinyurl.com/2hm3j5rn. Accessed on 10 April 2025.

17 Saran, Samir, 'COP27: India can't be expected to pay for climate sins of the West', *The Times of India*, 30 October 2022, https://tinyurl.com/4367py35. Accessed on 10 April 2025.

18 Ibid.

19 'ADB sets funding plan for Asia to combat climate change', *China Daily*, 2 May 2023, https://tinyurl.com/muevzyhn. Accessed on 10 April 2025.

20 'Rich nations pledge support for extra $200b in climate fund', *China Daily*, 23 June 2023, https://tinyurl.com/2s47r35b. Accessed on 10 April 2025.

21 As the IMF's Deputy Managing Director iterated in February 2023, just $630 billion a year in climate finance is currently being made available globally, with only a fraction of it going to developing countries. See 'Scaling up Climate Finance for Emerging Markets and Developing Economies', Speech by Deputy Managing Director Bo Li at EIB Group Forum 2023, 27 February 2023, https://tinyurl.com/5348wkun. Accessed on 10 April 2025.

22 Mohan, Vishwa, 'Require 42% cut in annual carbon emissions by 2030, says UNEP', *The Times of India*, 25 October 2024, https://tinyurl.com/34swsuxp. Accessed on 10 April 2025.

23 Ibid.

24 'Scaling up Climate Finance for Emerging Markets and Developing Economies', Speech by Deputy Managing Director Bo Li at EIB Group Forum 2023, 27 February 2023, https://tinyurl.com/5348wkun. Accessed on 10 April 2025.

25 Ibid.

26 Saran, Samir, and Mari Elka Pangestu, 'Setting a path to green, resilient and inclusive development', *Samirsaran.com*, 18 January 2022, https://tinyurl.com/47y9kmd6. Accessed on 10 April 2025.

27 'A New World: The Geopolitics of the Energy Transformation', IRENA, 2019, https://tinyurl.com/63d7tz8d. Accessed on 10 April 2025.

28 Ibid.

29 Yu, Yifan, 'AI's looming climate cost: Energy demand surges amid data center race', *Nikkei Asia*, 12 June 2024, https://tinyurl.com/yjardmmd. Accessed on 10 April 2025.

30 Ibid.

31 Ibid.

32 Ibid.

33 Ibid.

34 'Executive summary', *World Inequality Report*, 2022, https://tinyurl.com/5xn72wsd. Accessed on 10 April 2025.

35 Ritchie, Hannah, et al., 'CO_2 and Greenhouse Gas Emissions', *Our World in Data*, https://tinyurl.com/3ypchmrb. Accessed on 10 April 2025.

36 China today mines nearly three billion tonnes of thermal coal, and burns it cleanly as compared to India's 900 million tonnes which is used for generating 80 per cent of India's electricity. Coal consumption within the electric power sector in the United States fell to 387.17 million short tonnes in 2023. In the past decade, there has been a marked decline in the use of coal for electricity generation in the US, with coal consumption having peaked between 2005 and 2008 when over one billion short tonnes were used every year.

37 Wyk, Barry van, 'China's top 15 electric vehicle companies', *The China Project*, 18 May 2023, https://tinyurl.com/yeppnmsd. Accessed on 10 April 2025.

38 'Trends in other light-duty electric vehicles', *Global EV Outlook 2024*, IEA, https://tinyurl.com/2u6pbhyr. Accessed on 10 April 2025.

39 Myllyvirta, Lauri, 'Analysis: China's emissions set to fall in 2024 after record growth in clean energy', *Carbon Brief*, 13 November 2023, https://tinyurl.com/44uyjk3h. Accessed on 10 April 2025.

40 UNEP, *Emissions Gap Report 2024*, 2024, https://tinyurl.com/yn8pcmtd. Accessed on 10 April 2025.

41 Li, Cheng, and Xiuye Zhao, 'Renewable energy should not be the next semiconductor in US-China competition', Brookings, 14 June 2023, https://tinyurl.com/yxmhv7b5. Accessed on 10 April 2025.

42 Baskaran, Gracelin, 'Could Africa replace China as the world's source of rare earth elements?', Brookings, 29 December 2022, https://tinyurl.com/42jwfxsr. Accessed on 10 April 2025.

43 Victor, David G., and Michael R. Davidson, 'Accelerating the clean energy revolution by working with China', Brookings, 18 June 2024, https://tinyurl.com/3vmr675u. Accessed on 10 April 2025.

44 Song, Sha, 'Funding the green technology innovation pipeline: Lessons from China', World Economic Forum, 8 May 2024, https://tinyurl.com/2hm3j5rn. Accessed on 10 April 2025.

45 Ibid.

46 Ibid.

47 Ibid.

48 Gupta, Surojit, 'A new "arms race" is on among countries for critical minerals', *The Times of India*, 25 August 2023, https://tinyurl.com/y4wfey9v. Accessed on 10 April 2025.

49 'Key market trends', *Critical Minerals Market Review*, IEA, 2023, https://tinyurl.com/yn5k5324. Accessed on 10 April 2025.

50 According to the National Bureau of Asian Research's Special Report of December 2022, which examined the risks associated with the growing scarcity of critical minerals, 'The scramble for new mineral supplies and processing capacity is not taking place in a geopolitical vacuum.' This new geopolitics of clean energy is being shaped by intensifying strategic competition as well as recent shocks to global supply chains that are fundamentally changing the way that countries and companies organize their supply systems and production chains. Control over critical mineral supply, processing, and clean technology manufacturing has become a central element in the widening US-China strategic and economic competition. See Wu, Yu-Hsuan, and Phung Quoc Huy, 'Geopolitics of Critical Minerals', NBR Special Report 102, December 2022, https://tinyurl.com/3ehv9mrv. Accessed on 10 April 2025.

51 Victor, David G., and Michael R. Davidson, 'Accelerating the clean energy revolution by working with China', Brookings, 18 June 2024, https://tinyurl.com/3vmr675u. Accessed on 10 April 2025.

52 The US-Africa Leaders Summit of 2022 hosted by President Joe Biden was evidence of a US diplomatic-strategic make-up effort. After all, Africa's critical minerals could power America's green energy transition.

53 Nearly a decade ago, the Chinese initiated the annual China-Africa Heads of Summit State Summit—formally known as the Forum on China-Africa Cooperation (FOCAC). The last summit held at Beijing in September 2024 saw the presence of as many as 51 African heads of

state or government. Neither the US nor India have been successful in attracting this level of attention from African leaders. China has worked hard and long in fostering these relationships. See Singh, Ram, 'China-Africa Summit 2024: The Octopus' Embrace', *The Diplomat,* 12 September 2024, https://tinyurl.com/cvj66tv7. Accessed on 10 April 2025.

54 Schneidman, Witney, and Vera Songwe, 'Africa's Critical Minerals Could Power America's Green Energy Transition', *Foreign Policy*, 3 August 2023, https://tinyurl.com/3fncv8xs. Accessed on 10 April 2025.

55 For example, an Australian firm (Cobalt Blue) planning its first cobalt refinery in collaboration with Japan's Iwatani Corp. is going ahead with the project despite a massive slump in battery metal prices, betting that US and European efforts to break China's dominance in critical minerals will support alternative supply chains. See, Turton, Shaun, 'Australian cobalt refiner bets on demand for 'ethical' China-free EV metals', *Nikkei Asia,* 5 April 2024, https://tinyurl.com/3ruh92yr. Accessed on 10 April 2025.

56 'GDP per capita (current US$) – India', World Bank Group, https://tinyurl.com/485dabef. Accessed on 10 April 2025.

57 In PPP terms, India's per capita income was $1,204 in 1990, and rose about nine times to $10,176 in 2023. See 'GDP per capita, PPP (current international $) – India', World Bank Group, https://tinyurl.com/muetufc3. Accessed on 10 April 2025.

58 'Top 10 richest countries in the world by GDP per capita in 2025', *Forbes India*, 26 February 2025, https://tinyurl.com/bdfm2fs7. Accessed on 10 April 2025.

59 Sharma, Manisha, et al., 'Climate Change and the Indian Economy - A Review', *Current World Environment*, 2022, https://tinyurl.com/mr3fjn29. Accessed on 10 April 2025.

60 'The human cost of disasters: an overview of the last 20 years (2000–2019)', Centre for Research on the Epidemiology of Disasters (CRED), United Nations Office for Disaster Risk Reduction (UNDRR), https://tinyurl.com/4wfr9xvh. Accessed on 10 April 2025.

61 Roome, John, 'India seeks to arrest its alarming decline in groundwater', *World Bank Blogs*, 25 May 2022, https://tinyurl.com/2krxtsnu. Accessed on 10 April 2025.

62 Ibid.

63 Panja, Sumit, et al., 'Climate change impact on the coastal areas of India: A Review', Asutosh College, https://tinyurl.com/4vfnhub3. Accessed on 10 April 2025.

64 Mohanty, Bimal, et al., 'The Impact of Climate Change on Marine and

Inland Fisheries and Aquaculture in India', *Climate Change Impacts on Fisheries and Aquaculture*, B.F. Phillips and M. Pérez-Ramírez (eds.), Wiley, 2017, https://tinyurl.com/mtw88pda. Accessed on 10 April 2025.

65 Panja, Sumit, et al., 'Climate change impact on the coastal areas of India: A Review', Asutosh College, https://tinyurl.com/4vfnhub3. Accessed on 10 April 2025.

66 'The Water Future of Earth's "Third Pole"', NASA, https://tinyurl.com/hdt6pjkx. Accessed on 10 April 2025.

67 Saran, Samir, 'COP27: India can't be expected to pay for climate sins of the West', *The Times of India*, 30 October 2022, https://tinyurl.com/4367py35. Accessed on 10 April 2025.

68 The *Panchamrit* includes (i) reaching a non-fossil fuel energy capacity of 500 GW by 2030; (ii) fulfilling at least half of India's energy requirements via renewable energy by 2030; (iii) reducing CO2 emissions by 1 billion tons by 2030; (iv) reducing carbon intensity to below 45 per cent by 2030; and (v) achieving its net-zero emission target by 2070. See PIB, 'India is committed to achieve the Net Zero emissions target by 2070 as announced by PM Modi, says Dr. Jitendra Singh', Ministry of Science & Technology, Government of India, https://tinyurl.com/5258bezt. Accessed on 10 April 2025.

69 Chowdhury, Aditi Ray, 'With COP29 Underway, India's Road Ahead for 2030 Emission Targets Still Appear Bumpy', *Outlook Planet*, 30 October 2024, https://tinyurl.com/3tbezyb5. Accessed on 10 April 2025.

70 Critics, however, point out that the report ignores the fact that India's per capita emission is low at 2.9 tonnes of carbon dioxide equivalent (tCO2e), well below the global average of 6.6 tCO2e. See Chowdhury, Aditi Ray, 'With COP29 Underway, India's Road Ahead for 2030 Emission Targets Still Appear Bumpy', *Outlook Planet*, 30 October 2024, https://tinyurl.com/3tbezyb5. Accessed on 10 April 2025.

71 'Hydroelectric power projects with aggregate capacity of 15 GW under construction', Ministry of Power, 5 April 2024, https://tinyurl.com/289hxyxx. Accessed on 10 April 2025.

72 'National Green Hydrogen Mission', Ministry of New and Renewable Energy, Government of India, https://tinyurl.com/2z8fyebw. Accessed on 10 April 2025.

73 'Hydroelectric power projects with aggregate capacity of 15 GW under construction', Ministry of Power, 5 April 2024, https://tinyurl.com/289hxyxx. Accessed on 10 April 2025.

74 Ibid.

75 Ibid.
76 'Power Sector at a Glance "ALL INDIA"', https://tinyurl.com/4r6jtntf. Accessed on 10 April 2025.
77 Central Electricity Authority, Ministry of Power, Government of India, *National Electricity Plan, Volume II– Transmission*, October 2024, https://tinyurl.com/3pn87vva. Accessed on 10 April 2025.
78 'Surge in India's renewables tendering set to keep coal's share below 50% in total installed capacity', Institute for Energy Economics and Financial Analysis, 15 May 2024, https://tinyurl.com/5f6x97en. Accessed on 10 April 2025.
79 'Power Sector at a Glance "ALL INDIA"', https://tinyurl.com/4r6jtntf. Accessed on 10 April 2025.
80 Central Electricity Authority, Ministry of Power, Government of India, *National Electricity Plan, Volume II– Transmission*, October 2024, https://tinyurl.com/3pn87vva. Accessed on 10 April 2025.
81 'Power Sector at a Glance "ALL INDIA"', https://tinyurl.com/4r6jtntf. Accessed on 10 April 2025.
82 Central Electricity Authority, Ministry of Power, Government of India, *National Electricity Plan, Volume II– Transmission*, October 2024, https://tinyurl.com/3pn87vva. Accessed on 10 April 2025.
83 Bandyopadhyay, Krishnendu, 'IIT-Bombay prof on 11-year "energy swaraj yatra" aboard solar-run bus', *ET Energy World*, 15 July 2022, https://tinyurl.com/mu26r8cz. Accessed on 10 April 2025.
84 Sheng, Andrew, and Sneha Poddar, 'Lessons from Ladakh's climate leadership', *Inquirer*, 29 May 2024, https://tinyurl.com/yaahp67v. Accessed on 10 April 2025.
85 Wallace-Wells, David, *The Uninhabitable Earth: Life After Warming*, Tim Duggan Books, 2019.

Epilogue

1. Maddison, Angus, 'The World Economy', Development Centre Studies, Development Centre of the Organisation for Economic Co-Operation and Development, https://tinyurl.com/yby7v7wf. Accessed on 7 May 2025.
2 Lu, Marcus, 'Visualizing the Future Global Economy by GDP in 2050', *Visual Capitalist*, 22 August 2023, https://tinyurl.com/426vvtxv. Accessed on 7 May 2025.
3 'GDP per capita of India: Current & historical data (2015 to 2025)', *Forbes India*, 24 April 2025, https://tinyurl.com/2cbj4s3k. Accessed on 7 May 2025.

4 Baldwin, Richard, 'China is the world's sole manufacturing superpower: A line sketch of the rise', CEPR, 17 January 2024, https://tinyurl.com/4f3nfucy. Accessed on 7 May 2025. Further, when it comes to gross production, China's share is three times that of the US, six times that of Japan, and nine times that of Germany.

5 Nobel laureate Simon Kuznets is best known for the Kuznets' Curve which describes the relationship between economic growth and inequality.

6 As is well known, Bhutan has, for a long time, adopted the Gross Happiness Index as a measure of its societal welfare levels. President Nicolas Sarkozy of France, in 2008, commissioned a project on finding a more contemporary and relevant measure of general public welfare. This project was led by two Nobel laureates, Professor Amartya Kumar Sen and Professor Joseph Stiglitz. Their final report titled *The Measurement of Economic Performance and Social Progress Revisited* has not really received the attention it deserves, surely because of the reluctance of and the inertia in US-dominated institutions like the World Bank and the IMF which are currently perceived to be the guardians of global macroeconomic phenomena. See Stiglitz, Joseph, Amartya Sen, and Jean-Paul Fitoussi, 'The Measurement of Economic Performance and Social Progress Revisited', OFCE, 2009, https://tinyurl.com/2c8akzfd. Accessed on 18 April 2025.

7 The recent pronouncements of RSS Sarsanghchalak Mohan Bhagwat, who has repeatedly advised that there is no merit or purpose in looking for more temples under different mosques, need to be heeded.

8 The *Vishwamitra* terminology is borrowed, with gratitude, from Vallabh Bhansali. It is far better to aim to emerge as a Vishwamitra than a *Vishwaguru*; the latter sounds somewhat pompous, and certainly premature.

9 The sub-optimality is revealed in a simple comparison. India and China had very similar per capita incomes in 1990 (China $372, India $320). Today, China's per capita income at $15,300 is nearly five times that of India, which is at $2,940. At the time of Independence, India had a higher per capita income as well as foreign exchange reserves with the UK, which gave us the resources to build domestic reserves.

10 This system of assigning KRI to all covenanted officers, and making them accessible to the public will, it is envisaged, replace the system of annual performance reports (APRs), which has completely outlived its utility and become dysfunctional. With nearly 95 per cent of those being assessed securing 'excellent ratings' in their APRs, this system has become opaque, and prone to extremely subjective bias.

11 The proposed methodology goes beyond the operationalization of Constitutional Amendments 73 and 74. Institutional arrangements created under these amendments do not provide for establishing an accountability framework based on quantified KRIs.

12 The idea of a district-led development blueprint is inherent in the Aspirational Districts Programme (ADP) initiated by PM Modi, and operationalized for 112 districts by NITI Aayog. The goal was to achieve the national average level of human development indicators for all these 112 (effectively less developed) districts solely through improving the governance. Pahle India Foundation is one organization that is attempting to implement the district-led decision-making and development programme in Assam, supported by the Government of Assam. Madhya Pradesh is likely to be next. The objective is to finalize the template, and then scale it across the country to all districts.

13 Tiseo, Ian, 'GHG emissions in India - Statistics & Facts', *Statista*, 7 February 2025, https://tinyurl.com/4rp4k58e. Accessed on 7 May 2025.

14 'Energy-intensive economic growth, compounded by unfavourable weather, pushed emissions up in China and India', IEA, https://tinyurl.com/3rb6h8db. Accessed on 7 May 2025.

15 Ritchie, Hannah, and Max Roser, 'India: CO2 Country Profile', *Our World in Data*, https://tinyurl.com/mvvsyedz. Accessed on 7 May 2025.

16 'India's per capita emissions less than half of global average in 2022: Report', *The Economic Times*, 5 December 2023, https://tinyurl.com/2s38pw4d. Accessed on 7 May 2025.

17 Data is from the India Electricity Authority as reported on the NITI Aayog Energy Dashboard.

18 All figures on organic carbon content are from the ICAR-Indian Institute of Soil Science.

19 Figures taken from a presentation by Shri Gajanan Dange, president of Akshya Krishi Parivar, at the workshop on natural farming in Hyderabad.

20 'Fertiliser subsidy bill in FY'23 seen at Rs 2.3-2.5 lakh crore; may fall 25pc in FY'24: FAI', *Financial Express*, 6 December 2022, https://tinyurl.com/y43vz5wv. Accessed on 7 May 2025.

21 China, the world's largest emitter, did not commit any funding to the FRLD, but is reported to have provided substantial climate funding through its BRI. The US, which is the second-largest emitter of greenhouse gases, has committed a paltry $17.5 million. All this clearly demonstrates that advanced economies will not come to the aid of the countries in the Global South for helping with the mounting costs of

climate change. The World Bank, meanwhile, has been tasked to service the FRLD at a fee of 17 per cent!

22 Khadka, Navin Singh, 'How Trump's "drill, baby, drill" pledge is affecting other countries', *BBC*, 17 February 2025, https://tinyurl.com/37xpx7fv. Accessed on 19 April 2025.

23 Former Norwegian minister of the environment and international development, and executive director of UNEP, Erik Solheim makes a passionate argument that the US matters 'much less than we tend to think' when it comes to climate change action, even as he reiterates that the nation which, more than any other, caused the climate crisis appears on course to leave it to the rest of the world to sort out the mess. See Solheim, Erik, '4 Reasons Why the Climate Coalition Will Win Despite Trump', Inter Press Service, 12 November 2024, https://tinyurl.com/5fp8ujjs. Accessed on 19 April 2025.

24 Erlanger, Steven, and Christopher F. Schuetze, 'Split on Economic Policy Puts Germany's Government at Risk of Collapse', *The New York Times*, 2 November 2024, https://tinyurl.com/3me5pjuc. Accessed on 19 April 2025.

25 'Global Energy Market Outlook Hydrocarbon demand', Government of Alberta, September 2018, https://tinyurl.com/ms4374dp. Accessed on 19 April 2025.

26 'Median Age of India', database.earth, https://tinyurl.com/5xd3zxyc. Accessed on 7 May 2025.

27 'Number of employed persons in India from financial year 2018 to 2023, with estimated for 2024', *Statista*, https://tinyurl.com/5crfd87m. Accessed on 7 May 2025.

28 'Quarterly Bulletin', Periodic Labour Force Survey (PLFS), October–December 2024, https://tinyurl.com/26ujwr9z. Accessed on 8 May 2025.

29 International Labour Organization, *India Employment Report 2024*, 2024, https://tinyurl.com/azuwpddn. Accessed on 18 April 2025.

30 'Annual Survey Of Unincorporated Sector Enterprises (ASUSE) 2023–24', Ministry of Statistics and Programme Implementation, National Statistics Office, https://tinyurl.com/84bzkaf3. Accessed on 18 April 2025.

31 'Employment in agriculture (% of total employment) (modeled ILO estimate) – India', World Bank Group, https://tinyurl.com/3uzbcb2c. Accessed on 8 May 2025.

32 Nagaraj, R., 'What has "Make in India" achieved in the last decade: Data', *The Hindu*, 2 October 2024, https://tinyurl.com/yr4rrph6. Accessed on 8 May 2025.

33 'India's share in global trade doubled since 2005, comparatively

moderated in last 10 years: Report', *The Economic Times*, 26 December 2024, https://tinyurl.com/mvuj6nay. Accessed on 8 May 2025.

34 Pahle India Foundation is working with the state government of Uttar Pradesh to help design its export promotion policies. Districts with higher export propensity are being identified, and measures being designed, after consultation with the exporters, on achieving an exponential growth in exports from these districts.

35 'Govt to set up deregulation commission to further reduce State's role in governance: PM Modi', *The Hindu*, 16 February 2025, https://tinyurl.com/2p9j7nzw. Accessed on 8 May 2025.

36 High-level corruption and scams, which characterized the second term of the UPA government, have decreased under its successor regime. Here too, however, there is growing evidence of some large corporate houses using the 'agencies' to achieve business goals at lower-than-fair (market-determined) prices, and win government tenders. This also discourages honest private sector entrepreneurs to plan future investments.

37 PIB, 'India's Ranking in Travel and Tourism Development', Ministry of Tourism, Government of India, 1 August 2024, https://tinyurl.com/52wvkyem.. Accessed on 18 April 2025.

38 'Over 18 mn int'l tourist arrivals in 2023: Centre', *The Economic Times*, 26 December 2024, https://tinyurl.com/3f9nxe9z. Accessed on 8 May 2025.

39 A recent paper by the Economic Advisory Council to the Prime Minister (EAC-PM) puts the number of total migrants at about 400 million, and it seems to have marginally declined in recent years. These would include all migration related to marriages and inter-district migration, and not necessarily the number of workers who move from their place of work to their homes each year.

40 Sporadic but deadly violence against migrants in cities like Mumbai and Bengaluru is evidence of the social stress that is already visible. It also becomes a handy political tool which can threaten societal peace and stability.

41 'Dropout Rate by Sex and Level of School Education in different years', Ministry of Statistics and Programme Implementation, Government of India, https://tinyurl.com/mrjjsevd. Accessed on 8 May 2025.

42 ASER, *Annual Status of Education Report 2024*, 2024, https://tinyurl.com/3y9eppxk. Accessed on 8 May 2025.

43 'Gross enrolment ratio for higher education only 28.3% in the country, goal is to improve it to 50% by 2035: AICTE Chairman', *The Hindu*, 29 June 2024, https://tinyurl.com/4vkb4724. Accessed on 8 May 2025.

44 Roy, Annapurna, 'How India is Using the Internet', *The Economic Times,* 10 March 2024, https://tinyurl.com/y92fksxk. Accessed on 18 April 2025.

45 'Ministry of Education releases All India Survey on Higher Education (AISHE) 2021-2022', Ministry of Education, Government of India, https://tinyurl.com/ycts97vy. Accessed on 8 May 2025.

46 These universally credible statistics are provided in the Government of India's Ministry of Health publication *National Family Health Survey (NFHS -5) 2019–2012,* published in 2021. See the Compendium of Fact Sheets, India and 14 States/UTs.

47 Srivastava, Varnika, 'Who has maximum gold in India? Who owns 22579618 kg gold in the country', *DNA*, 8 January 2024, https://tinyurl.com/224p4jpx. Accessed on 8 May 2025.

48 Menon, Raja, 'Reorienting Indian Military Grand Strategy Defensive Territoriality to Offensive Oceanic in the Indo-Pacific', https://tinyurl.com/3npyzdsu. Accessed on 18 April 2025. Menon, Raja, 'How India's new naval base at Andamans will force Beijing to reassess its strategy', *The Indian Express*, 14 March 2023, https://tinyurl.com/yckyseym. Accessed on 18 April 2025.

49 The apprehensions of respected security analysts about a two-front military threat from China and Pakistan in the early 2000s led India to develop a strategy based on deterrence and dissuasion to prevent any loss of territory (sadly, without resourcing the military adequately). See Singh, Sushant, 'The Challenge of a Two-Front War: India's China-Pakistan Dilemma', *Stimson*, 19 April 2021, https://tinyurl.com/37n25jab. Accessed on 18 April 2025.

50 Ibid.

51 But, as Raja Menon pithily puts it, what the Indian Army is fighting is geography, not so much the Chinese. See Kaushik, Krishn, 'Rear Admiral Raja Menon: "What the Indian Army is fighting is geography, not so much the Chinese"', *The Indian Express*, 17 January 2022, https://tinyurl.com/4avjwjkm. Accessed on 26 May 2025.

INDEX